Out of Mighty Waters

Out of Mighty Waters

Sermons by African-American Disciples

Edited by
Darryl M. Trimiew

Chalice Press
St. Louis, Missouri

Biblical quotations, unless otherwise noted, are from the *New Revised Standard Version Bible*, copyright 1989, Division of Christian Education of the National Council of the Churches of Christ in the USA. Used by permission.

Cover design: Anna Bryant
Art Director: Michael Dominguez

10 9 8 7 6 5 4 3 2

Library of Congress Cataloging–in–Publication Data

Out of mighty waters : sermons by African-American Disciples / edited by Darryl M. Trimiew.
    p. cm.
   ISBN 0-8272-2708-6
   1. Christian Church (Disciples of Christ—Sermons. 2. Sermons, American—Afro-American authors. 3. Afro-American Christians (Disciples of Christ)—Religious life—Sermons. I. Trimiew, Darryl M., 1952-   .
   BX7327.A1098 1994
   252'.066'08996073—dc20   94-26372

Contents

He reached down from on high,
he took me;
he drew me out of mighty waters.

Psalm 18:16

Introduction

Darryl M. Trimiew

African Americans have been an integral part of the Christian Church (Disciples of Christ) from its inception as the coalition of two early nineteenth-century frontier evangelistic movements under the joint leadership of Alexander Campbell and Barton W. Stone. Unlike other religious bodies that were established in the Old World, the Disciples began on the North American continent. Though most often as slaves, African Americans were nevertheless charter members in this worship of God.

Black Disciples were initially sequestered in slave galleries. Rarely did they take communion with their masters. But even so, they celebrated the Lord's Supper and soon began preaching. Ironically, one of the earliest Black Disciples ministers was Alexander Campbell—no, not Thomas Campbell's son but the *other* Alexander Campbell, the Black one, who in 1834 was ordained and pastored a Black congregation, Midway Christian Church in Midway, Kentucky. From this early beginning, many African-American ministers have followed in Campbell's footsteps. Their contributions to the church have been invaluable.

1

This volume is a collection of some of the best current sermons from within that tradition. Black Disciples have never been as numerous as Black Methodists or Baptists on a national level, but our influence has not been negligible. Indeed, our presence in regional areas has been impressive.

Our reputation as preachers in the African-American chanted sermon tradition has been somewhat obscured by our location in a predominantly European-American denomination. Thus, Black Disciples preachers have been enmeshed in a classic catch-22 situation. Essentially ignored in books on homiletics and sermon collections compiled and edited by European-American Disciples colleagues, we have also failed to be acknowledged by our Black ecumenical partners in predominantly Black denominations. They have been, quite naturally, preoccupied by their own preachers, their own sermon series.

That we have our own outstanding preachers has never been doubted, however, in the Black community. Our common thematic thread has been a dedication to evangelization, to spreading the gospel of Jesus Christ, and to the uplift of humanity—in particular, the uplift of the African-American community. And like other Disciples, we have made contributions to the cause of ecumenicity.

But no collection of sermons can tell a whole church's story, and this collection is no exception. This volume is designed to fill us with the awe and presence of God that is always present when the gospel of Jesus Christ is preached. With that goal in mind, this collection works admirably. The quality of sermons is matched only by the great variety of topics. From Texas storytellers to urban raconteurs, nearly every Black preaching style may be found here.

Like previous collections of sermons from the Black churches, much of the excitement and aesthetic values of this complex performative art form is lost in the translation of the preached sermon to the cold printed page. One cannot experience the radiance of authority that shines forth on the face of a Magdalen Shelton as she preaches, nor the reflected radiance on the faces of her rapt congregation as they listen: their moon to her sun. Nor can the towering figure of an Alvin Jackson with his arms outstretched like some great bird of prey be captured on paper, even in the considerable power of his words. Equally elusive is the wise pulpit presence of an

Ozark Range, holding forth like an ancient African griot whose sophistication must be personally experienced to be adequately appreciated.

This inability to re-present these sermons in all their power, this unavoidable loss, is a sad yet inescapable reality that presented the editor of this volume with a dilemma. Should such gems be presented in a manner in which much of their luster cannot be seen? Or, should the gospel legacy that Black Disciples have set forth simply be left to the memories of those who heard them preach, and enter into legendary status for their successors? I have opted for the former course. Too much of Black history has been lost, too much legacy mislaid. That their full aesthetic power cannot be reduplicated adequately is a limitation that simply must be accepted.

But just possibly, even in manuscript form, much of the power, entertainment, holiness, and deep psychological and spiritual insight remains. Like the roar of a waterfall or a mighty river, the power of these sermons lives on after the preaching event. As reservoirs of God's Spirit in this world, their preservation and presentation here allows them to be held in reserve, their power like dammed-up water, ever ready to burst forth on a dynamo—spinning new human wheels of endeavor, inspiring new converts, ministers, and Disciples.

Accordingly, these sermons burst forth not as the vibrant call-and-response, electrifying soul chants that some of them manifested in their original incarnation. This second coming into print is not the Victoria Falls, the mighty waters pulsating in the heart of Africa. These sermons come from a greater distance. In their written form they have been subtly subdued. But their diminishment is an odd phenomenon. *Out of Mighty Waters* is authentic, catalytic, and mesmerizing. Like a mighty waterfall that is a mile beyond your view, you can still hear their deep roar and sense their awesome power without actually being on the spot, or under the cascade. Indeed, to experience all these sermons as they were preached—by some special intervention of God in which the hearer could move instantaneously from one rapture to another—would, like the cascade of a real waterfall, prove to be an experience too dangerous and too powerful. One might see visions, like John at Patmos.

Thus, although this collection is something of an echo, it is nonetheless a powerful echo. These preachers' voices sing out, sometimes in crescendo, sometimes in diminuendo. Like great recordings of jazz, these sermons have layers of meaning, hidden rivulets of nuance and insight. And, in their written form, like majestic rivers they can be rafted and ridden again and again. A first reading of some of these sermons is like a first river run in which the happy sailor thinks that she or he has survived an adrenaline-pumped white-water ride. Yet even after this virgin voyage, these sermons remain unexhausted. There are deep pools here, heavily shaded with the trees of wisdom planted nearby. Such beauty and repose that may be found there cause one to linger. Such peace causes one to reflect on the goodness of the Christian life even among the challenges of the rapidly moving world. Linger with some of these sermons and know once again that God has come to bind up the brokenhearted, and to quell the anxieties of the worrisome. Jesus is the Master of the storm on the tempestuous seas of trouble.

In an age of disintegrating families, storms are raging. Thus, a few concluding remarks are in order. A major tributary in this collection is the theme of Christian responsibility, and though each sermon has its own distinct emphasis, responsibility dominates. John Compton's "Benbow Family Reunion" helps us reevaluate what we have lost in our rapid-transit, frozen-pizza, post-modern world—a world where we live so far apart that a telephone company has more emotionally effective ads for us to "reach out and touch someone" than do many of our churches. Thus, Compton's sermon calls us to a renewed expression of Christian responsibility as was manifested in the traditional African-American extended family. A similar call to responsibility comes from Delores Carpenter's "Bridging the Chasm" and T. Garrott Benjamin's challenging focus on the plight and promise of young Black men. Richly laced with humor, L. Wayne Stewart's "Changing Shoes" also echoes powerfully the call to responsibility in a way that is profoundly disturbing.

These sermons need no further introduction. They are ready to live again. They speak for themselves out of a wisdom, power, and spirit of love that will become obvious to you as you savor them. With a great deal of joy I call you to come alive as you sip from the pure springs of the gospel, *Out of Mighty Waters*.

$\mathcal{A}$ Call to Serve

Walter D. Bingham

Walter Bingham, a native of Memphis, has retired
after many years of service in nearly every capacity for
the Christian Church (Disciples of Christ). He is a
graduate of Howard University Divinity School and
served for many years as pastor of Third Christian
Church in Louisville, Kentucky. A pioneer in
race relations, Walter was the first
African-American moderator of the
Christian Church (Disciples of Christ).

Mark 1:16–20

As Jesus passed along the Sea of Galilee, he saw Simon
and his brother Andrew casting a net into the sea—for
they were fishermen. And Jesus said to them, "Follow
me and I will make you fish for people." And immediately they left their nets and followed him. As he went
a little farther, he saw James son of Zebedee and his
brother John, who were in their boat mending the nets.
Immediately he called them; and they left their father
Zebedee in the boat with the hired men, and followed
him.

The call of the first disciples by our Lord and Savior, Jesus
the Christ, Son of the living God, is a dramatic event in faith
history. As told by the Gospel of Mark, the call and the acceptance were instant, without prior acquaintance or prepara-

5

tion. The event was an act of faith. Considering the nature of the call and its demand to leave a present situation to enter a mission that required sacrifice and the risk of life, it could be described as a "leap of faith."

These first disciples left their vocation of catching fish to become fishers of people. Subsequent calls by Jesus elicited immediate affirmative responses from persons of diverse background—even a tax collector who was an agent of an oppressive government, imperial Rome, and one who would later betray the divine mission.

According to the Gospel of Luke, the total of the followers of Jesus eventually numbered one hundred and twenty persons, including women. The company of followers of Jesus included marginalized persons, outcasts, and those from whom he cast out evil spirits or healed from dreaded diseases. Some were those looking to be liberated from Roman oppression and were also rejected by the Jewish establishment. Some saw in Jesus one who would restore political power. None recognized, at first, his role as the Christ who would save people from their sins, or the person who by his resurrection from the dead would be the way for eternal life for human beings.

This diverse group of disciples could not and would not know until later the true mission of this prophet-teacher, nor the dimension of faith that would be required of them to "fish for people," to make disciples, "to take up the cross daily," to deny themselves, and to give their own lives for the sake of the good news of God's coming kingdom.

In the face of great uncertainty in following one who had no place to "lay his head," what was it about this man and his mission that captivated the first disciples? The answer is the key to understanding why, through centuries, women and men live to the call to servanthood to God in Christ Jesus.

Remember that in the time when persons accepted the call of Jesus to proclaim God's good news, there were many movements soliciting followers. Some were religious in nature, but still others were philosophical, political, cultic, and monastic in nature. Within Judaism itself, there were diverse groups promoting many different teachings and interpretations of the Law of Moses. The Pharisees and the Sadducees come readily to our minds.

Many diverse leaders, prophetic and charismatic, attracted followers looking for answers to fill their need for a change in their situation. People then and now were looking for liberation, healing, security, and salvation.

The early disciples came to discover in Jesus of Nazareth God's initiative of love for them and promise of salvation. When we accept discipleship in response to God's love, we learn why disciples in every generation have responded with utmost faith, hope, and love to the call of mission and service to all persons.

We now know that God has called us through Jesus Christ to his divine purpose. We know as did our predecessors that Jesus demands all that we are and all that we have to offer in gratitude for the high privilege of servanthood to God in Christ Jesus.

God's call to us comes directly to our very nature as mortal beings. It satisfies our longings, it evokes our response of praise and gratitude, and it empowers us to assume our role as his faithful servants.

The miracle of the calling of the servants of God in Christ Jesus suggests three thoughts.

First, we need to hear quite clearly the "voice" of God. The "voice" of God is, of course, "a divine sound in the ear." It is like no other sound we hear. It is like, perhaps, a sound intended only for the ears of the one receiving the divine call. It reminds us of what the boy Samuel heard and his mentor, Eli, didn't hear. Again, it is like the still small voice that Elijah heard following the mighty wind, the earthquake, and the fire. And still again, it could be like the voice coming from the unconsumed burning bush that launched the leadership of Moses and the Exodus from Egypt.

Perhaps, it is like the voice that Paul heard and his companions could not hear in his call on the road to Damascus. Perhaps it is a voice of sheer silence—so silent that even in the midst of loud and thunderous noise only the one being called really hears it. Finally, it could be a growing "sound in the mind" so persistent that one responds as Samuel eventually did: "Speak, Lord, for your servant hears." However the call comes, our response must be: "I will go where you want me to go, I will do what you want me to do, and I will be what you want me to be."

Second, the call to servanthood to God in Christ Jesus involves being a herald of God's good news, telling of his

loving mercy and warning of his judgment on those who rebel
against his commandments. We need "words for the mouth."

Words are important. Proclamation is essential in communicating the good news, the gospel. Servants of God in every
generation have been unsure of their ability to use words with
conviction and persuasion. They have been reluctant to take
on speaking tasks. The fear of embarrassment and rejection
coupled with shyness has often been too much for them to
respond to the call to proclaim "thus says the Lord," or "this is
the word of the Lord."

All servants of God, I believe, have great uncertainty about
their ability to speak for the Lord. This is quite understand-
able. It is an awesome assignment. No one should feel worthy
to assume the role of messenger for God. It has been and is a
humbling experience. It is possible only in the care and power
of the Holy Spirit. One should approach this task with prayer
and supplication.

Thank God, proclaiming God's good news is a task for all of
his servants: lay and clergy; women and men; young and old;
and all races of people in every nation and culture.

Know that we must proclaim God's good news when the
hearers reject and even kill the prophets. Know that they may
destroy the messenger but not the message!

When God sends you forth in the name of Jesus, go out in
joy, speak boldly, have no fear—for the God who sent you on
this journey of faith will go with you. He will empower you
with every ability you need. Remember, Jesus said, "When
they bring you before the authorities, don't worry about what
you will say, the words will be given to you." I believe that the
power of the Holy Spirit will give us "the words in the mouth"
that we need.

The charismatic gift of the use of words for communicating
the gospel must be cultivated and strengthened by homiletical
study, theological research and reflection, and serious biblical
study. Style and skill in communication are a necessary tool
in a word for the Lord. Then there are those unique gifts of
personality and persuasion given to us by God that individu-
ally identify each servant of God.

Two stories illustrate the power of preaching the Word as
a result of theological and homiletical training together with
unique gifts often associated with ethnicity. The first one
concerns an African-American minister who, after years of

preaching, decided on his sabbatical to take a course in homiletics at a nearby seminary. When he returned from his leave, he told his waiting congregation what he had learned about sermon preparation and delivery. He said, "I learned that every sermon has three sections: the introduction (exegesis, background and interpretation of the text of scripture); the development or exposition of the theme; and the conclusion, which includes the appeal to respond to the message. It's that final part that appealed to me. You and I call that section the 'Arousement.' And since you and I understand that all too well and since I know what you like, I'll skip the first two parts and proceed on to the third part."

The second story concerns an intentional movement to draw together the churches and members of a racially mixed neighborhood to become better acquainted with each other. After a series of exchanging preachers and members, after a period of time one White minister made the following observation: "If we could just combine the brevity of White worship with the fervency of African-American worship, it would improve our Sunday morning attendance wonderfully."

Use the words in your mouth given to you by God as you serve in Christ's name.

Finally, we need a song in the heart and movement in the hands and feet for the task of servanthood to God in Christ's name. A song in the heart is a sense of praise and joy in deepest gratitude for what the Lord has done. The songs of the heart express our joy, our faith, our hope, and our love for the God who first loved and our love for our sisters and brothers who share also his rich blessings.

There are certain situations when our songs of the heart may be difficult to sing. Sometimes they come forth as laments, as the "blues," as a consequence of despair, agony, and deep suffering. Captive Jews in the sixth century B.C. cried out in protest when their captors commanded them to sing their songs of faith: "How can we sing the LORD's song in a foreign land?" (Psalm 137:4).

But the Spirit of the Lord God is upon us and we must sing our "hallelujahs" and "Amens."

African-American slaves, despite the harshness of their circumstances, found a way as chattel slaves to "lift every voice and sing," to steal away to Jesus, to look toward heaven and sing "over my head there must be a God somewhere," and to anticipate the coming of God's kingdom on the earth, bringing liberation of their physical bodies and salvation to their souls.

With our hands and our feet, we are empowered by God's Spirit to be "salt to the earth" and "light to the world." Let us accept with faith, hope, and love our call to serve. The word of the Lord, Amen.

$\mathcal{B}$ridging the Chasm

Delores Carpenter

Delores Carpenter is pastor of Michigan Park
Christian Church in Washington, D.C., and associate
professor of Christian education at Howard University
Divinity School. Holder of several degrees, including one
from Howard Divinity School, her doctorate in education
is from Rutgers University. In 1994, *Ebony* magazine
listed Delores as one of the best
Black preachers in America.

Luke 16:19–30

A stellar member of our basketball team was shot in the head and killed in July 1993. Something must be done and done quickly about such violence in our land. These are like the days of Noah when violence corrupted the earth.

The rich man of Luke 16:19 ignored the beggar Lazarus when Lazarus sat at his own front gate. He found himself in the place of torment when he died. He looked up and saw Lazarus resting in the bosom of Abraham. What separated them was an uncrossable chasm.

It's ironic what can happen to us when we fail to watch what's happening at our own front gate. We too are creating a seemingly uncrossable chasm between the haves and the have nots, between those who have gotten it together and those who are still stumbling in the dark, between those who feel liberated and those who feel hopelessly trapped, between the church and the unchurched, between the middle class and the underclass.

I wonder if Lazarus was sitting there in the crowd when Jesus said, "Blessed are you who are hungry now, for you will be filled."

Obviously the rich man was not. I wonder what message the rich man wanted Lazarus to take back to his brother. Of this I am certain: it would address the grievous consequences of ignoring the poor.

This parable makes it plain that even God has a deadline. And when we reach God's deadline, we must give an account of the stewardship of our lives. You remember that other parable of the unjust steward, which appears right above this one in the same chapter. The unjust steward was known to have resources. He was from a nice family who set him up in business, but he never learned to work. When his poor management practices were uncovered, he tried to position himself so that he wouldn't have to work and he won't have to beg. He said, "I'm too ashamed. I'm not going to be a bagman. I'm not going to sit on the corner with a cup." He negotiated unfair deals with his master's debtors, hoping that when he lost his position, they would welcome him into their homes so that he could sponge off them. But making friends with dishonest wealth could not save him. His shrewdness in the money matters of this world could not save him. And Jesus says this is because you cannot serve God and money; you must be devoted to one and despise the other. It doesn't mean you can't have money. It means that if you do have wealth, you've got to work hard to convince God that you love God more than you love your money.

And if we cannot do this, we will be like the rich man, one upon whom the resurrection was wasted. If the gospel works its full measure in us, we will learn to be more concerned for others and especially the poor more than we care for ourselves. What the church does with her resources is the measure of her faith. What a nation does with its resources is the measure of her greatness. Hoarding capitalists are bad stewards.

This is true in part because wealth is often divorced from virtue—even prudence, thrift, or frugality. Wealth is not always a badge of intelligence, character, wisdom, fortitude, or honesty. In a money economy, your assets have nothing to do with your behavior, or whether you needed it or deserve it. Instead money makes money, the rich get richer, and the poor get poorer. Money made in dealing drugs and guns leads to the destruction of individuals, families, and whole communities. Yet most drug dealers and gun dealers do not seem to be ashamed of the money they make. They spend freely. Not too many seem to be working hard for their wealth.

The only test that seems to count is how much money you can get for doing the least amount of work. America's obsession with soap operas such as *Dallas, Knots Landing, Dynasty,* etc., depicts a culture of the leisurely rich who hardly work or don't work hard. And whenever wealth is devoid of work, compassion, faith, and wisdom, God can't get through. And the seemingly uncrossable chasm between the rich and the poor remains uncrossable. In this kind of climate, the resurrection is a wasted accomplishment.

The rich man tells Jesus that if someone who is raised from the dead would go back and warn his brothers, they would change. But Jesus refutes this assumption and in so doing pays those who proclaim God's truth the greatest of compliments. He says if they will not hear the prophets, they also will not listen to one who is raised from the dead. This should give those who teach a social gospel special reassurance. For he is saying that if they do not hear you, they will not hear him—the one God raised from the dead. He is saying that we as a nation, and as a global village, already have heard enough truth to be convinced and to have a change of heart. But we know that the human heart is deceitful and stubborn. And until we want to believe, God must wait.

In the meantime, the Bible does its best to make us hurry up. It says we must worry about the things that are unjust right now so that we can keep our minds on our work and throw off everything that hinders us in the struggle against evil. Then we can throw everything that we have into the fight. Today, it is a fight against violence, guns, homicide, and megapoverty. This wide gulf sometimes allows us to glaze over our eyes, so that we are insensitive to the vast poverty that exists throughout our world.

The economic empowerment agenda and the nonviolent agendas have not progressed sufficiently in our church. We are like Moses looking at a burning bush that will not consume itself. We are standing before the burning bush of poverty and the burning bush of violence. But, unlike Moses, we have not yet realized that we are standing on holy ground. We just want to be spectators when God wants to get us involved in slaying the giants that keep on coming. God wants to move us to an activist position. We can start with our urban areas that the church has almost totally abandoned. And I know that God wants to take us into the city and God wants us to get up and go quickly. This is vividly portrayed in Acts 12:10, which says, "They came before the iron gate leading into the city. It opened to them of its own accord, and they went outside and walked" down one street.

This text appears in the story of Peter's liberation from prison. Herod, after seeing how well the Jews responded to the death of James, arrests Peter with the idea of killing him after the Passover, before a large delegation of people. He built their hopes up to expect another execution during this festival of unleavened bread. Peter, whose hands are chained, falls asleep between two guards. With a great light an angel comes and tells Peter to "get up quickly." Peter was asleep and all obstacles to his freedom are removed as he puts on his belt, ties his sandals, and wraps his cloak around him. Not the light, not the angel, not that Peter thought he was seeing a vision, not that he had to get dressed first, but of most interest to me is *where* the angel takes him. God could have lifted Peter up and sat him down in Mary's house, safe and secure. But God took him to the streets of the city.

And that's exactly where God wants us to go as a church today—in order to regain space and an abiding place, a sanctuary for God among his people there. For the city is one of the great intersections of rich and poor, powerful and powerless—across the crowded roads of life with many different cultures, languages, and beliefs rubbing shoulders with one another. The city is where we can begin to bridge the great chasms of shelter, health care, security, and food. Here is where Jesus again wants to minister to his people and we are the instruments of his reconciling presence. But we must first hear him calling us there. "When he calls me, I will answer, When he calls me, I will answer, When he calls me, I will answer, I'll be somewhere, I'll be somewhere listening for my name." I'll be somewhere working for the Lord.

Second, we must go *quickly*. Too often we hesitate, wondering if we can make any difference at all, wondering if we can stay with the urban agenda long enough to see change, wondering if it's worth all our efforts. Perhaps this story can help to motivate us:

On Christmas Island in the Indian Ocean, south of Java, one million crabs try to procreate. Each November they travel by land to deposit their eggs. Many are crushed by cars; one hundred thousand make it to the shore. Males and females mate. The females climb up on the cliff overlooking the ocean. They watch for the tide to come in. At the proper time, they climb down to the shore to deposit their eggs in the water. It is a delicate balancing act for them to shake themselves vigorously, while they dig their claws into the sand for grounding. At the same time that the tide washes over them, they release their eggs to be carried out into the sea. Each female sheds one hundred thousand eggs and hopes that she will not be carried out in the ocean with the eggs, because these crabs cannot swim. Many of them die in this process.

Of the eggs that are carried to sea, many are eaten by the fish soon after they hatch. Few are able to reach land to assume their final adult form. The vast majority never do. But enough make it to continue the species. Extravagant—this planting of seeds, but successful for their survival.

We must be willing to be just as extravagant in the seeds we plant in ministry. Some of the poor are in our midst, sitting beside us each Sunday. We should be careful how we treat those in our own midst who have the least. When we go to the city, we must examine the stewardship of our own resources. We must determine whether or not we are straddling the fence regarding how our Christian commitment stacks up against our love of money. We must loosen our tight grip upon materialism in order to receive the riches of God. We must be ready to declare with the hymn writer William Newell:

Years I spent in vanity and pride,
Caring not my Lord was crucified,
Knowing not it was for me he died, on Calvary.

By God's Word at last my sin I learned,
Then I trembled at the law I'd spurned,
Till my guilty soul imploring turned to Calvary.

Now I've giv'n to Jesus everything;
Now gladly own him as my king;
Now my raptured soul can only sing of Calvary.

O, the love that drew salvation's plan!
O, the grace that brought it down to man [sic]!
O, the mighty gulf that God did span at Calvary!

Who can bridge the gap? Who can span the chasm? Who can remove the distance?

Jesus is his name. And the reason I know he can is because he has done it again and again. In Luke 7:22 he answered John—the blind receive sight, the lame walk, the lepers are cleansed, the deaf hear, the dead are raised, the poor have good news brought to them. If he did it two thousand years ago, he'll do again today.

And lest you are not yet convinced that he can close the chasm, that he can bridge the gap, that he can remove the distance, let me tell you my story. One day I was across a chasm far away from God. It seemed uncrossable, unbridgeable, and unspannable. But *Jesus* did what the law could not do. *Jesus* reached down to me. Jesus looked beyond my faults and saw my need. *Jesus lifted me up* to where I could hear God, feel God, and sense God. Now, if he could do that for me, Jesus can break every evil fetter, save every hopeless soul, and deliver every drug dealer. Jesus can save every fragile family and heal every broken heart.

Jesus can make every promise of God real to his people. The ones who want to get over, can get over. The ones who want to get back home, can get back home. The ones who are poor can have both the material and spiritual riches of God.

Because Christ Jesus bridged the chasms of our lives, he can increase our faith and trust in order that he may use us in this great work of peace and reconciliation.

$\mathcal{T}$he Storms Are Raging

Raymond L. Brown

Raymond Louis Brown is the pastor of East Second
Street Christian Church in Lexington, Kentucky. He is a
graduate of Jarvis Christian College and
Phillips Graduate Seminary.

Luke 8:22–25*

Storms are raging. Are you anchored in the Lord?

We have come here this week facing the reality that the storms of life are raging across our nation and world with a fierceness that suggests the convergence of opposing fronts. The searing heat of urgency to redeem the social and political economic plight of our communities collides with bitter cold winds of racism and injustice that never seem to abate. These are not just isolated and separate occurrences. Upon the landscape of human activity and interaction these storms are developing along well-defined lines of frustration and futility everywhere.

---

*The scripture references in this sermon are from the King James Version of the Bible.

17

The storms from so volatile a condition, even as we speak, are gaining momentum of strength against the days and the times. Our great concern is that many of us are living in a place where there seems to be no obvious shelter. No hope for tomorrow. No dream worth dreaming. And no nourishing well that cherishes life and the living. Storms of life are raging all around us. They are raging in presidential politics, raging in Supreme Court decisions, raging in assaults against morality, and raging in the civil strife that any and all of us must endure. The storms are raging in Los Angeles and in New York. Storms are raging in Chicago and in Miami; in Philadelphia and in Cleveland storms are raging. But the storms are also raging in Lake Edna and in your neck of the woods.

But in the midst of these storms we have also come here to celebrate our tradition in the good news that there is a word from the Lord. Our tradition is pregnant with rich imagery and the theology that has arisen out of our own personal identification with life's temptations, trials, and tribulations. It is a tradition pregnant in imagery that portrays all life's turmoils, whatever the shape they take. It is the result of intercourse with the transcendent and indefatigable dynamism of an almighty and sovereign God. In the perpetual motion of time that is the days of our lives, by the fashion and construct of the mind, heart, and will of God, there is a visitation upon the world. There is a visitation to which we have given ourselves willingly, openly, and freely in a love relationship. And we understand that with ultimate superiority, with omnipotent ability and eternal presence, God is God— and without partiality, because God is no respecter of persons. The storms of life are raging and are raging upon the just and the unjust alike.

Yet children of the Heavenly King—children of the Heavenly King know who they are and whose they are and so they speak their joys abroad. Children of the Heavenly King know that this is not their home and so they can sing the Lord's song in a strange land. Children of the Heavenly King have their "hope built on nothing less than Jesus' blood and righteousness." And so they can theologize "like a ship that's tossed and driven, battered by an angry sea when the storms of life are raging and their fury falls on me. I wonder what I have done that makes this race so hard to run. Then I say to

my soul, take courage, the Lord will make a way somehow"
(Thomas Dorsey).

And so we don't give up and we don't give in. We don't back
down and we don't back away. We press and fold our fear and
faith but we keep on believing and we keep on trusting. We
keep on praying and we keep on praising. We keep on singing
and we keep on theologizing about the good news that is our
hope, even in the midst of the storm. But in the midst of the
storm, that's the crux and the crucible, that's the critical point
and the utmost test. In the midst of the storm—ahh, the storm
is raging; ahh, the storm is bringing all of its fury to bear; ahh,
the storm is unleashing its worst with catastrophic potential,
with unrelenting force and magnitude, in danger and darkness—in the midst of the storm, *is your hope anchored in the
Lord?*

Hope is a challenging course and a prophetic word for the
church in the 1990s. Hope is a prized possession and a privileged position that the church has been oblivious to but in
whose descent is the Spirit. Hope is one of the charter members of the high court of heaven, a star in every crown and the
stuff without which salvation is not complete. Hope is a judg-
ment-day catalyst that has no equal. Hope is the positive
superlative eager to inhabit every soul. Hope is a doorway
without a door, a statute without limitations, a stronghold
unmoved and a pathway unrolling to eternity. Its master and
maker is God; its tutor and benefactor is Christ; its transportation is the Holy Ghost and on the wings of the wind its
destination is this world—*Is your hope anchored in the Lord?*

I have to pose that question tonight because of an acute
sense that maybe the church's fate in the nineties will be that
we have not seriously wrestled with the genuine need for a
concise witness to the spirituality of hope—the abiding presence and help of hope, the redeeming and liberating power of
hope. When it ought to be our crowning achievement too many
are wallowing in the shelterless pits of despair, having given
up on hope because what they have come to know of hope was
not the answer.

It does not make any sense to me that people would have
no hope; no, it doesn't make any sense at all. But the record
will show that the burden for a defining witness was with the
church and in that we will be judged. But I know that there is
still hope for the church. Yet a fundamental flaw again is that

we have not connected with the true and living hope, the one and only hope. Check it out. Jesse has been out there, a prophetic voice, crying in the wilderness, as if hope was in danger of dying. But the problem is not that hope is dying, because hope is on the Lord's side. The problem is that there has not been a witness to define effectively, to proclaim outstandingly, the manifestation of the Spirit that enables us to take a somersault of thought into the inconceivable in order to stand in the presence of the power and protection of God.

Let me unpack that a little bit. I like Luke's text because Luke allows me the opportunity this evening to see the underlying structure of the text and we've got to dig down into it. The underlying structure reveals that for the disciples it was inconceivable that Jesus had done what he did. They did not even have a frame of reference. They could not get their minds around, they didn't have a notion, they could not get it in their heads, that Jesus did what he did in rebuking the storm. But even more than that, what they marveled at was the fact that once Jesus rebuked the storm, the storm obeyed. And then they were more afraid of the manner of man than they had been at their own thoughts of perishing in the storm.

You see, what we must learn is that hope is a spiritual principle under the unction-anointing and amazing grace of the Spirit. It is not just an innocent and idle bystander in the trilogy of faith, hope, and love, but it carries its own weight as a miraculous and mysterious, beautiful movement of the Spirit. It's not just something that you take lightly. Lord, I hope that these storms don't last much longer. But hope is spiritual grace that can be actively brought to bear in any situation and put to good use like nothing else can. *Webster's* defines hope as confidence—expectations to look forward to with the confidence of fulfillment. Yet when the Spirit descends to take us up sailing away, the best of our hope just seems to be earthbound. We are coveting a shadow when the real thing is within our grasp.

For instance, right now, we are hoping that Bill Clinton becomes the next President of these United States. Hope is that a change will cause the sun to shine and move out some of these dark clouds that have been hanging over us. But you see, we ought to know better. We ought to know better. It's still the White House. I don't care who you put in it, it still the White House!

Our hope is too earthbound. Jesus asked these earthbound disciples, "Where is your faith?" And even by definition the answer requires a somersault of thought, for what is faith? "Faith is the substance of things hoped for, the evidence of things not seen" (Hebrews 11:1). Hope is in God. "Eye hath not seen, nor ear heard, neither have entered into the heart of man, the things which God hath prepared for them that love him" (1 Corinthians 2:9). Where is your faith? I tell you, the answer to the question really is another question: Why did you not act in the certainty of fulfilling your own hope? Why did you not act with confident expectation in your God? Why did you not rebuke the wind and command that there be peace in the midst of the storm? Am I getting through? You see, if we back up just a little bit more we can see the real issue is not so much that in the midst of storm we've got to wake up Jesus, but because we are asleep—and sometimes with our eyes open—Jesus has got to wake *us* up!

Jesus has got to wake us up because the substance of our hope has just been a flickering flame rather than a burning fire shut up in our bones. But when the substance of our hope reaches the place where the power of the Spirit can work in us; when the substance of our hope has been rightfully joined to faith and love in the way, the truth, and the light; when the substance of our hope has taken a somersault of thought into the inconceivable, then shall the world have a true witness, then shall our hope be truly anchored in the Lord, then shall all the world know it for what it is and see it and live.

As long as the church is in the world, there is no reason why any in the world should be without hope. I like the way Paul puts it in that eighth chapter of Romans (verses 18–19) where he says, "For I reckon that the sufferings of this present time are not worthy to be compared with the glory which shall be revealed in us. For the earnest expectation...waiteth for the manifestation of the [children] of God." The writer of 1 John put it another way: "Beloved, now are we the [children] of God, and it doth not yet appear what we shall be: but we know that, when he shall appear, we shall be like him; for we shall see him as he is."

And even David, way back there in the Twenty-seventh Psalm, knew exactly what hope is all about. You know how the Twenty-seventh Psalm starts out:"The LORD is my life and my salvation; whom shall I fear? The LORD is the strength of my life; of whom shall I be afraid?" And then it ends up saying, "Wait on the LORD: be of good courage, and he shall strengthen thine heart: wait, I say, on the LORD." But don't you know that on the way from light and salvation to waiting on the Lord, David says in that next to the last verse, "I had fainted, unless I had believed to see the goodness of the LORD in the land of the living"? I had fainted; I had given up all hope. I had just as well lain down and died except that I believed that I would see the goodness of the Lord. You see, behind every bend in the road, I expected to see the goodness of the Lord. Around every corner in every situation, no matter what the crisis, no matter what the problem, my earnest expectation was to see the goodness of the Lord.

I wish I could take you a little bit farther. But you see, I've come to the place where I've had to set my anchor, hoping against hope. You see, I've already taken my somersaults of thought. That's why I can tell you about it, and I'm hoping against hope—in other words, I will persist in hoping even against all odds. I hope in hope even if it's wrong. I hope in hope even if it tears me apart and sends me all the way where I cannot tell. I hope against hope because I know that hope is the true and living word of God that shall never fail. Hope is that which teaches us about heaven. Hope is that which teaches us about salvation. What do you think Paul was talking about in that eighth chapter of Romans (verses 24–25) when he said "We are saved by hope: but hope that is seen is not hope: for what a man seeth, why doth he yet hope for? But if we hope for that we see not, then do we with patience wait for it." And that takes us right back to David saying, "Wait on the Lord."

Wait on the Lord. If you know the Lord is gonna be good, wait on him! If you know that even in the midst of the storm the Lord is gonna make a way somehow, wait on him! Don't give up. Hope says if you'll just hold out till tomorrow, if you'll just keep faith through the night, if you'll just hold out till tomorrow, everything—everything, everything, I don't care what it is, everything, because of the expectation that God will do something good, everything—will be all right! Everything will be all right.

In your churches where you've got problems, where Satan has got on you and won't get off, remember that the Lord is good, that he'll deliver you. And you know something? You can take hope and you can whip the devil upside the head all day long. After a while he'll get tired of it because, you see, he's the one that's got no hope. He's the one.

Well, at any rate, we have a mission and we have a task, for we have the goods. We have the hope, a God of hope, a Lord of hope, a Spirit who expressly brings unto us the hope of every generation. And so, if there are people out there in the world who have no hope because of their situation, it's because we have not done what we have been called to do. If there's no hope out there in the world because they can't put up with the storms of life, it's our fault because we have not communicated the truth that the rains of heaven are still falling on the just and the unjust alike. And if you're in the storm, that means I'm in the storm too. And if we're both in the storm, something's wrong if I'm looking for the goodness of the Lord and you're not.

We've got a message and we ought to proclaim it. We are the witness of the truth of hope, the goodness of hope, the liberating power of hope. Hope will set you free. So I want to call you to this ministry. I want to call you to this very thing that has set the good news on fire—for, you see, had it not been for the Lord on our side, had it not been for the fact that he went to the cross, had it not been that he decided to die for your sins and for my sins and for all the sins of the world, had it not been that on that cross he did die, there would be no hope. There would be no hope, but you see, he had hope. Ah-ha, that's why he could go to the cross. He knew that even around that corner he could expect the goodness of God to intervene and extract him even from the worst situation! And so three days later, three days later he got up singing, "I'll fly away, O glory, I'll...."

That's our Lord of hope, whom we have joined ourselves to. The message is simple. Let us serve him in the hope he has given us.

*J*esus Calming the Storm

Robin E. Hedgeman

Robin Hedgeman serves as associate regional
pastor of the Christian Church in Ohio. She is a graduate
of Towson State University and Lexington Theological
Seminary. Ordained in 1988, Robin previously pastored
Howett Street Christian Church in Peoria, Illinois. She
has just completed a term as chair of the board of
directors of the Division of Overseas Ministries of the
Christian Church (Disciples of Christ).

Mark 4:35–41

Our theme for this week has a text that can be found in all three of the Synoptic Gospels—Matthew, Mark, and Luke. However, it seems to me that Mark includes some vivid details that seem to suggest an eyewitness report.

The text informs us that, as Jesus and his disciples were getting away for some rest and had started across the Sea of Galilee, a storm of great turbulence broke loose and their boat nearly capsized. Galilee was a sea notorious for sudden storm attacks.

Jesus and the disciples were heading toward the east side to the region of Gerasenes. He had experienced a long and busy day. He had taught a mass of people, argued with the scribes, and explained some parables to the disciples. Jesus needed to get away from the crowd. The scriptures tell us that he decided to get a little rest, or "R and R," as we need to do every now and then.

24

The disciples, who consisted of several experienced fishermen, took charge of the voyage. I'm certain that just as Jesus went into a deep sleep and really began to rest and perhaps start dreaming, that was the moment that he was awakened. The dream and the journey were interrupted by a sudden furious squall, common on this lake.

For, you see, the lake was surrounded by high hills and narrow valleys that functioned as wind tunnels. And a storm in the evening was especially dangerous. On this occasion, the boisterous waves broke over the boat so that it was nearly swamped.

Can you imagine their fear as this happened? They were not traveling in one of those luxury liners we take cruises on. They did not even have a motor in their boat, just a sail to propel them. They did not have life jackets, or shortwave radios to send an SOS signal for help. All they had on board was Jesus and he was stretched out, sleeping as if he did not have a care in the world.

Sure, he was exhausted from a full day of teaching. But how could he rest so well, asleep in the stern of the boat, with all that thundering noise, and the fearful disciples pondering about him?

Mark says the panic-stricken disciples woke him and said: "Teacher, do you not care if we perish?" And it is only in Mark that we find this accusation that Jesus did not care if the disciples were about to drown. The implication being made here is that if Jesus cared, then he would do something. He would save them. He would get them out of the awful predicament they found themselves in.

The crises that you and I face reveal some of the same characteristics faced by the disciples. And sometimes we, also, think that Jesus is sleeping. What do we do when our loved one is diagnosed as having cancer or AIDS? When the contract where you work is not renewed and you are laid off, wondering how you will make ends meet, let alone pay the mortgage? We also want to know, "Jesus, are you sleeping? Do you not care if we perish?"

That relationship that promised to have been made in heaven ends, and once again your heart has been broken. We then also wonder, "Jesus, are you sleeping? Do you not care if we perish?"

When the storms of life toss us to and fro, we feel just like the disciples. They wondered to what degree Jesus really cared.

I imagine it must have been an awesome storm to give the disciples cause to worry. After all, some were experienced fishermen. They knew their trade inside and out. They knew that rain would come with a west wind and heat with a south wind. They were so good at understanding weather signs that Jesus must have wondered why they couldn't interpret the signs of their present time.

The disciples were keenly familiar with the waterway. They knew a squall could quickly erupt on the horizon and spread over the entire lake. They were not novices; they knew what could happen. Still, when the storms of life started threatening, they panicked. They could see only death and doom in front of them.

When we are confronted with a crisis, no matter how prepared we may be, the sudden onset brings fear and despair. The disciples quickly became frightened as the storm intensified. Their boat began to fill with water. The real danger of sinking became apparent. They didn't know what was going to happen to them. They could not even think straight because of their fear.

You know how it is when fear is clouding your mind. Just think about all the drugs and gang violence that run rampant in our communities. Fear causes us not to be able to deal with it. We are afraid to come out at night, afraid to get involved, afraid to call the police, afraid to put our drug-addicted relative out of the house and into a recovery program. When fear strikes, our minds get cloudy and we just can' t seem to think straight.

And as the fear escalates, it turns into despair. The disciples felt despair as they realized their boat was sinking, just like the sinking feeling some of us get in the pits of our stomachs as we realize things are going from bad to worse.

The disciples were feeling pretty desperate. And they thought that Jesus did not even seem to care. They cried out, "Teacher, don't you care if we drown? Wake up, Teacher, and do something!"

Although the disciples called him "Teacher," they had not fully grasped his teachings. They did not recognize the power of the one they called Teacher. Even though Jesus had healed withered minds, withered bodies, withered souls, and withered hands, they still did not understand what it meant to be in the presence of Jesus.

There are times when we are in difficult situations and God is silent and seems to be absent. We pray but seem to get no answer. We then begin to ponder: Where is God? God, don't you care about our plight?

God, don't you care if the Rodney King verdict made the Dred Scott decision seem like a landslide victory? At least Dred Scott was determined to be three-fifths of a man. But Rodney King seems to have received less than humane treatment.

God, don't you care that Black America is in intensive care? All kinds of addictive behaviors have infiltrated our communities. Every eight seconds of the school day, a Black public school student is suspended. Every day one Black child under five years old is murdered in America.

The world around us is in intensive care. In southern Africa most of the male population who are employed are migrant workers. In Zaire there is a four-digit inflation rate, and in Central Africa AIDS is prevalent and rampant, killing our people. Lord, don't you care?

Storms are raging all across the world. There is poverty and strife, drought and famine, economic and political conflict. It becomes difficult to understand and even more difficult to explain the crises of life.

One moment everything is going great; the next moment the storm winds begin to blow, and our world is sinking around us. That's when we begin to call out just like the disciples: "Lord, don't you care if we drown?"

During these times we need to be reminded that when Jesus awoke, he rebuked the wind and said to the sea, "Peace! Be still!" At this command, the wind ceased, there was a great calm, the waves were muzzled, and the lake became completely calm.

My mother used to teach me that every shut eye ain't asleep and every good-bye ain't gone. What manner of man was this? He really wasn't sleep. And the psalmist assures us, "Behold he who keeps Israel will neither slumber nor sleep."

Jesus then rebuked his disciples for being afraid in a crisis. Despite Jesus' teaching, it still had not dawned on them that God's authority and power were present in Jesus. This is what he meant by his second question, "Why are you afraid? Have you still no faith?"

In stilling the storm Jesus assumed the authority exercised only by God in the Old Testament. Perhaps that is why the disciples were terrified. But when they saw that even the forces of nature obeyed him, they must have been in awe and amazement. For they then asked one another, "Who then is this, that even wind and sea obey him?"

Here in the state of Ohio, we have become personally acquainted with storms and wind and rain this summer. For about the last few weeks we have had tornado warnings, thunderstorm warnings, and a few flood warnings.

Sometimes the weather forecaster has been accurate and other times not too accurate. I don't know what kind of radar system your forecaster uses, but we have something called the Doppler system. Well, the Doppler radar has interrupted many television programs to show us the direction of the storm, how fast it is moving, and where it is coming from.

Weather reporters and forecasters do their best to report the information, but sometimes they miss the mark. Radio and television stations sometimes assure their listeners that their weather reporter carries the seal of approval from the National Weather Service. I suspect the people of Jesus' day would certainly have qualified for this seal of approval without all the advanced radar systems.

The weather is very much with us. We have acquired more sophisticated instruments to predict the weather than those present in Jesus' day. But, I wonder, are we more prepared for the storms?

Jesus performed miracles out of his deep and constant concern for persons. His love and his empathy with those who suffered compelled him to provide healing and wholeness. Wherever possible, he ministered to those in need and those who were hurting. Among the many deeply moving passages of the Gospels is the description of Jesus weeping beside the tomb of Lazarus, sharing grief with Mary, Martha, and the others, the grief of their loss. Jesus performed miracles not simply to proclaim who he was but because of his great love and compassion for persons.

This evening I just want you to know that even though I'm no weather reporter and I do not have any special radar system to predict the direction of your storm and although I do not have the seal of approval from the National Weather Service, you need to get anchored because *storms are going to come.*

I know I do not stand alone as one who has experienced some storms!

We've seen the lightning flashing
And heard the thunder roll
We've felt sin's breakers dashing
Which tried to conquer our soul
But then we heard the voice of our Savior
He bid us still fight on
He promised never to leave us
Never to leave us alone.

I believe that while we're trying to get anchored we might need to make a few phone calls and be reminded of the love of Jesus Christ.

I don't know who you would call but I would call Paul and say, "Paul, what can you tell Disciples in Cleveland, Ohio, gathered at the twelfth biennial session of the National Convocation about storms?"

And I believe Paul would say, "Now, Hedgeman, I don't have any of that modern technology used by weather forecasters in Cleveland." He would go on to say that the National Weather Service has not granted him the seal of approval. "But I am acquainted with storms from personal experience," he would tell us.

He would begin with an inquiry: "Who will separate us from the love of Christ? Will hardship, or distress, or persecution, or famine, or nakedness, or peril, or sword?" Then he would go on to say, "No, in all these things we are more than conquerors through him who loved us. For I am convinced—I don't know about you, but I'm even confident; I don't know about the state of your soul but I am absolutely, positively sure—that neither death, nor life, nor angels, nor rulers, nor things present, nor things to come, nor height nor depth, nor anything else in all creation shall be able to separate us from the love of God in Christ Jesus our Lord."

And then when I hung up from Paul I'd go back in time and call up Noah. I believe Noah would say, "Disciples, I don' t have any kind of advanced radar system and I do not have the seal of approval from the National Weather Service; but I too know something about storms."

He would give us a personal testimony about love in the midst of the storms. He would tell us that one day God sent a

storm into his life. It was not a little storm but a big storm.
The storm was so big, in fact, that it rained forty days and
forty nights. So devastating and destructive was the force of
the storm that the animals could only get on board two by two.
Noah would even tell us that "God so loved me that he sent me
a dove to let me know that the flood was over and told me: No
more water, but fire next time."

And then I would call Jonah and say, "Jonah, what can
you tell Disciples about storms?" I believe he would say, "I
don't even have access to the radar systems and no one has
given me any seal of approval, but...."

He would say, "I didn't expect a storm that day I left the
port of Joppa on a luxury liner bound for distant Tarshish.
There were blue skies and a cloudless horizon when I left; but
I ended up in the belly of a whale before I got to where I was
going." He would even tell us that "because of God's love, God
spoke unto the fish and it vomited me out upon the dry land."

This love that I'm talking about is not one of God's majestic attributes but the essence of God's being.

Ask Mary and Martha to stop by the Grand Ballroom at
the twelfth biennial session of the National Convocation. I'd
say, "Mary of Bethany, what can you and your sister Martha
tell us about love in the midst of the storm?"

I believe they would tell us that their storm occurred when
Old Man Death came knocking at their door and took away
their brother Lazarus. Upon seeing Jesus, Martha said, "Lord,
if you had been here, my brother would not have died. He's
been dead now for four days." Jesus said, "Tell me where
you've laid him." He then raised Lazarus from the dead and I
believe Mary and Martha could testify about love in the storm.
They would tell us that their brother who was once dead is
now alive.

God is Love.
Love is of God.
Love comes from him because it is in him.
God is love's prime fountain.

This love that I'm talking about is *agape* love. That's a
voluntary, active kind of love. This love links God and person
and unites soul and soul in a divine communion. It's a love
that runs deep. Runs from heart to heart. Breast to breast.

It's a love that informs us that, even though you are in intensive care and life support systems are nearby: "Church, we have the key to the future. We can determine our own destiny."

Problems aside, the Black church is the strongest and oldest institution left in our inner city neighborhoods. We just need to return to our history. For more than two hundred years the Black church has faithfully served the neighborhoods. We have been centers of celebration and rejuvenation.

Hardships of the past have compounded our problems to this present state.

But don't quit in the storm. Stay on the boat.

Don't give up in the storm. Stay on the boat.

Don't jump overboard with the first wind that slaps you in the face. Stay on the boat.

Don't abandon your life vest, don't lower your sail, don't cut off your engines, and don't participate in the mutiny of self-destruction. Stay on the boat.

It's an old ship, a leaky ship, a weather-worn ship, but it's a good ship. Somebody said it's the old Ship of Zion. But it's landed many a thousand. All you need to do is get on board.

Jesus will meet us and tell us:
Ain't no danger in the water.
Just get on board.
It will take you home to glory.

*J*ust Shake It Off

James L. Demus, III

James Demus is pastor of Park Manor Christian
Church in Chicago, Illinois. He is a graduate of
McCormick Theological Seminary in Chicago. This
sermon was preached on November 7, 1993,
at Mississippi Boulevard Christian Church in
Memphis, Tennessee.

Acts 28:1–5

To each and every one of you who are my Father's children I greet you in the name of our Lord and Savior, Jesus Christ.

As I look around this beautiful church and this tremendous congregation I'm reminded of the story that I heard told once of a pastor who visited one of the families in the church unexpectedly, and prior to his getting there they had been taking in very strong drink. When he knocked on the door they said, "Who is it?" "It's the pastor." They began to strut around trying to find an adequate place to hide this strong drink and so someone stumbled upon the idea, "Well, let's just put it in this carton of milk. He won't know the difference." Sure enough, as the pastor came in and visited with the family he said, "Would you happen to have a drink of milk?" And they looked around at one another and got him a tall glass of milk. The pastor looked at it and tasted it and then guzzled it all down without taking a breath. And as they looked at him with held breath they said, "How do you like the milk, pastor?" And he said, "My God, what a cow!"

As I look around this church, I'm saying to myself this morning: "My God, what a church!"

Just to remind you once again of our passage of scripture this morning: We're talking about the twenty-eighth chapter of the book of Acts, the first through the fifth verse, wherein it reads, "After we had reached safety, we then learned that the island was called Malta. The natives showed us unusual kindness. Since it had begun to rain and was cold, they kindled a fire and welcomed all of us around it. Paul had gathered a bundle of brushwood and was putting it on the fire, when a viper, driven out by the heat, fastened itself on his hand. When the natives saw the creature hanging from his hand, they said to one another, 'This man must be a murderer; though he has escaped from the sea, justice has not allowed him to live.'" Our verse of emphasis this morning is right here, wherein it states that Paul "shook off the creature into the fire and suffered no harm."

Paul shook off the snake into the fire and suffered no harm. For the time that is mine this morning I want to preach to you from a sermon entitled "Just Shake It Off." Just shake it off. Let us pray:

O God, wonderful Lord and Master, once more again it is that we come to you attempting to preach your Word. We know, Father, that it cannot and it will not and it shall not be done without you, so we're making an appeal right here and right now for you to participate in the process. Father, put volume in my voice, put Spirit in my speech, put truth in my talk in order that your will may manifest itself in this word. Father, unstop a deaf ear, open the closed eye, melt the hard heart in order that this word might find a place on fertile ground. In other words, Father, make the words of my mouth and the meditations of our hearts be acceptable in thy sight, O Lord, our strength and our Redeemer. Let the people of God say "amen" and "amen."

As we look and chew on this passage of scripture this morning, we find the apostle Paul and his shipmates having just been shipwrecked on an island called Malta. And even though they had just experienced the hair-raising experience and life-threatening ordeal of their ship running aground, crashing off what might have been a coral reef, our passage of scripture finds them safe and sound on shore, standing on solid ground—which is where many of you may be this morning as you sit comfortably in the pews.

You may have just gone through some kind of storm in your life that has wrecked your ship, that rocked your boat, that wrecked your world, that caused your day-to-day routine to be temporarily thrown into total chaos. It could have been an automobile accident, it could have been a death in the family, it could have been the loss of your job, but whatever it was, the Lord kept you. God protected you. God saw you through and even though your life has been shipwrecked you find yourself now safe on solid ground.

Paul reports to us that as they stood on the shores of that island the islanders *showed them unusual kindness.* The King James Version of the Bible says that those islanders were "barbaric," meaning that they were unchristian folk, but they showed Paul and his shipmates no small kindness, meaning that they were good to them. They were hospitable to them. They were kind to them. And isn't it interesting, my brothers and sisters in Christ, that folks outside the church can sometimes be kinder to you than folks inside the church? Here we are supposed to be of the household of faith—born of his Spirit, washed in his blood, talking about how this is *my* story and this is *my* song—yet many times the people in the world will be better to you than people in your own church. I point that out to you this morning because Paul seems to be wanting to make it clear to us that even though they may not be saved, there are still some kind folks out there. And if the Lord allows me to see how kind they are and you can show them something in return, you can do that by leading them to Christ! Then there'll be more kind, saved folks in the world. I'm tired of reading about how God has to wrestle people to the ground, how he has to put them on beds of affliction and all the time break them before they can be saved. Somebody needs to come because of the kindness of their heart.

Paul was on that island and it was raining and it was cold and out of the kindness of their hearts the islanders built them a fire. The islanders built them a fire. And as I read that word and meditated that word and prayed on that word, it came to my mind that we, as the church of God in relationship to the Spirit of God—we ought to be *on fire*. We should be on fire. I'm not talking about emotional whims that blow to and fro, with the coming and going of every latest religious fad. I'm talking about a spiritual fire! I'm talking about that something way down deep on the inside of you that'll make you *shout* when nobody else is shouting, that'll make you laugh when everybody else is crying, that'll make you dance when nobody else is moving, that'll make you cry when everything is gay, and make you feel good when everybody else is depressed. *That* fire! That fire that can have the wind blowing on the outside but keep you warm on the inside. That fire that a lot of us never get a chance to feel a part of because we're too busy running after other fires. I'm talking about the fire that comes from God.

I notice here that it says that Paul was gathering sticks to put in the fire in order to make the fire hot. Paul was gathering kindling to place in the fire in order to make it burn bright. Paul was placing wood in the fire to keep the fire going—which lets us know this morning that if we're going to keep the spiritual fires going we've got to continuously feed it. How do you feed your spiritual fire? Well, every time you come to a Sunday school class or a Bible study group, you're feeding your spiritual fire! Every time you read the word of God you're feeding your spiritual fire! Every time you give a tithe, you're feeding your spiritual fire! Every time you attend a prayer meeting, every time you say a prayer for somebody—give a praise report, testify to what the Lord has done for you in your life—you're feeding your spiritual fire! Every time you sing a hymn of praise, perform a work for the Lord, turn the other cheek, forgive and forget, serve and sacrifice, fast and pray, you feel those prayers wheels turn and your fire starts burning. Just a little talk with Jesus makes it right. *Feed* your spiritual fire.

But then you know you've got to be careful. When you start getting your fire going, first of all you've got to make sure that somebody else doesn't try to put your fire out. You've got to be careful of that. And the second thing is that you've got to be careful about the various kinds of people and things that are drawn close to you trying to receive the benefit and the warmth and the heat that your fire is generating. We came here this morning looking to have a hot time in the Lord, but you've got to be careful because every now and then, snakes come in the midst of trouble. In the midst of cold and rainy weather, snakes have a tendency to come from underground and sneak up and lay themselves by your fire. You see, snakes are cold-blooded creatures. They can't naturally warm themselves, so whenever their senses feel heat they go toward the heated area. They crawl up around a fire, roll over on their backs so that their bellies can be warmed.

What I'm trying to tell you this morning, church, is that when you decide that you're going to take God seriously, when you decide that you're gonna quit playing church, when you decide that you're gonna let God's Spirit penetrate your cold and calloused heart, when you decide that you're gonna give yourself totally over to Jesus and let your light so shine, the devil will send a snake out of nowhere that will try to put your fire out. Listen to the conversation of a snake. "Aw, baby, come on, you don't have to be that holy. Aw, baby, come on, you can miss Bible study just this one evening. Aw, baby, come on, you go to church every Sunday, why don't you spend Sunday with me sometime?" That's the conversation of a snake. Snakes always want to enjoy the warmth of your fire, but they don't want to contribute anything to keep the fire going.

As we see Paul stoking the fire, as we see Paul feeding the fire with wood, as we see Paul doing that which we ought to be doing to keep our fires going, the word of God says that a snake jumped up and bit him on the hand. It was a venomous snake. It was a poisonous snake. It was a deadly snake that leaped up and fastened itself onto Paul's hand. And let me tell you something, snake bites usually allow you to stand there for a minute or two before you drop dead from their poison; and the islanders who were standing around watching all of a sudden changed their attitude toward Paul. Originally they were very kind to him, but when the snake fastened itself to his hand they began to say that this man must be a murderer for such a bad thing to have happened to him, and it is justice that has caused him not to live.

But little did they know that God works in mysterious ways his wonders to perform. When it looked like the snake bite was going to destroy Paul, the reality was that the result was going to be altogether different from what they had expected. Look what happened while they were standing around talking, saying, "He must be a murderer, he must not be living right"—or that this is some kind of a divine payback for some wrong he has done—waiting on him to die. And I don't care who you are this morning, my brothers and sisters, whenever misfortune falls on you, rest assured there's always going to be some folks standing around waiting on you to die. Right now, right now, some of your "friends," some of your associates, even some of your family, are waiting on you to die.

But Paul gives us this morning the secret and the spiritual message of how to deal with snakes in our lives in all kinds of situations. Paul looked at the snake hanging on his hand and he heard the murmuring of the crowd standing around looking at him, waiting on him to die, and all of a sudden Paul just...shook it off. Did you hear me? He just...shook it off. There wasn't a whole lot of incantation, not a whole lot of buildup, not a whole lot of foolishness, not a whole lot of ritualistic gyrations—*he just shook it off!* He didn't go through any hollow prayer talking about how we're the army of the living God at whose command we bow, heart of the host that crossed the flood, we're the part that's crossing over. He didn't do all of that, *he just shook it off!* He didn't have to go through a whole lot of ritual, he didn't have to go through a whole lot of trouble, because he realized that some situations happen in your life that God might use them as a witness for somebody else. He didn't have to go through a whole lot of things, *he just shook it off!*

Well, there may be some of you here this morning who've got some people in your lives that need not be there; some of you this morning who've got some habits in your life that you need not have. There may be some of you here this morning who are walking down roads that you have no business walking on; and some of you here who've got hang-ups, all bound up where you can't get free. But I'm here to tell you this morning that the Master of heaven and earth, the sovereign Lord Jesus Christ, His High Holiness our Lord and Savior Jesus Christ, told me to tell you to quit making excuses about it, quit talking about what you can't do if you're in that kind of predicament—go ahead and *just shake it off!* I don't know about how you feel about it this morning, but whenever God gives you the power to shake things off you ought to go ahead and do so. Whether it be a snake, whether it be a habit, whether it be troubles, trials, and tribulations, you've been crying about that problem long enough. Now get up, wash your face and *just shake it off!*

What's that you say? That the death angel has visited your house? You can't seem to get grief and anxiety and depression that accompanies death off your back? Well, let me just tell you what Jesus did when death jumped on him one day and then I'll take my seat. You see the powers that be thought that if they would just crucify Jesus, that if they would just railroad him through their courts, if they would humiliate him in the streets, if they would just beat him in the back with their whips, pierce him in the side with their spear, nail him to the cross with their hammers and nails, crown him with a wreath made of thorns, mock him with their tongues and make him suffer until he died, that they would be through with him. That would be all that they would have to deal with Jesus. And death grabbed hold of Jesus and held onto Jesus all Friday. Death held onto Jesus all Saturday and Saturday night long, but early Sunday morning you tell me, what did he do? *He just shook it off!* He shook off death. He shook off hell. He shook off the grave. He shook off sin. He shook it off in order that we might have life again—*Jesus shook it off* and he shook it off forever.

I'll tell you this little story and then I'm through. A man had an old goat that stumbled one day into his dried-up well. And when he stumbled into that well the man tried to get the old goat out by dropping him a rope, but he couldn't get the goat out. He tried to pull the goat out, he reached at him, but he couldn't get the old goat out. So finally he decided, "Well, since I can't get him out, I'm gonna just bury him. He's gonna die anyway." And so the man began to shovel dirt on the back of the old goat, and every time he shoveled some dirt on the old goat's back, the goat would just shake the dirt off from his back and prance it down with his feet, and the more he shook the dirt down the more the goat would prance it down until finally the goat began to build an incline and he just walked out of that grave!

I want to let you to know this morning that you can shake it off, you can walk up higher and higher and higher. Can the church say, "Yes?" Can the church say, "Thank you, Jesus?" Can the church say, "Amen?" Let me put it the way the rap singers put it, "Just shake, sh-shake, shake, shake, *shake* it off."

Praise his name. Glory to God. What're you going to do? Shake it off! Hallelujah. Just shake it all off and walk it on down. Rise higher and higher.

*W*hat Are You Expecting for Christmas?

Lawrence A. Burnley

Lawrence Burnley is a Disciples of Christ campus
minister at the University of Pennsylvania. Larry has
degrees from the University of Cincinnati and Christian
Theological Seminary, and is a doctoral candidate at the
University of Pennsylvania.

Matthew 11:1–6

His name was John and they called him the Baptizer. He was the one who dared to speak out against those who were in power and oppressed the children of God. This was the one who called on sinners to repent of their sins. One could say that during his wilderness ministry John was in a season of advent, for he was preparing for the coming of the Messiah.

According to today's scripture lesson, John now finds himself in prison. We know that during this time sinners continue to sin, and King Herod, who arrested John, remains on his throne. As for John, the one who was obedient to God, he remains in prison.

While in prison John hears about the deeds of Christ. Jesus is healing the sick and giving sight to the blind. But back in Matthew 9:12 Jesus is hanging out with tax collectors and sinners of all sorts. I imagine John also heard about this.

John was no doubt baffled and anguished about his predicament of imprisonment and this news he's hearing about Jesus. Given these circumstances John would likely entertain questions such as, "Why is Jesus hanging out with sinners while I sit here in prison?" and "Why does oppression continue even after the Messiah has come?"

John was so confused and distraught that he asked his disciples to go and ask Jesus this question: "Are you the one who is to come, or shall we look for another?" Now surely *John* didn't ask this question. If anyone knew who Jesus was it was John. This is the same John who asked *Jesus* to baptize *him*. This is the same John who witnessed the Holy Spirit descending upon Jesus like a dove, the same John who heard a voice from heaven say "this is my beloved Son with whom I am well pleased." But after all this confirmation and affirmation, John begins to doubt his own witness. Why? Because the Messiah did not fulfill John's expectations. Jesus didn't come in with troops and weapons and overthrow the oppressor. As a result John begins to wonder if he had made a mistake. "Are you the one who is to come, or shall we look for another?"

I must admit that I am disturbed by John's doubt and if I could talk with John today I'd be compelled to ask him this question: "John, what were you expecting for Christmas?"

As we prepare for the coming of the Christ child in this season of Advent, I often hear these words of invitation: "Come, Christ, come." I submit to you this morning, church, that I am curious and concerned. The question that I would pose to John I pose to you: "What are you expecting for Christmas?"

To those of you who upon hearing this question begin to think about that coat you've been wanting, or that stereo you've been dreaming about, I say to you that you are totally missing the point of Christmas. You see, Jesus is the reason for this season.

My question this morning is directed at those of you who, like John, expect God to do something special and something powerful in and through the Christ. My question is also directed at those who sit on the fence contemplating the acceptance of Jesus the Christ as your Lord and Savior. I want you to be clean. I ask you, "What are you expecting for Christmas?"

Are you expecting God in and through Christ to come and solve all of your problems? Are you expecting the Wonderful

Counselor to remove your addiction to alcohol or drugs or to straighten out your marital problems? Do you expect God to miraculously put the church finances in the black? Perhaps you expect the Prince of Peace to wipe out AIDS or put an end to racism and sexism. Maybe God will clean up the environment or end world hunger and homelessness.

If you are expecting these types of gifts for Christmas, I'm afraid you are in for a big disappointment. Do not expect God to do what we must do for ourselves. If you have these types of expectations, confusion and doubt will begin to plague you and, like John, you may find yourself asking the one you call Lord and Savior, "Are you the who is to come, or should I look for another?"

I think it is sad that many Christians today believe that God has all the power. When things go wrong and we're confronted with some tragedy, we say, "It's God's will." Since God has all the power, God will make everything all right in God's time. We say that all this suffering and destruction in the world are a part of God's divine plan for salvation. It is a mystery. This type of understanding of the gospel does only one thing. It removes all responsibility from ourselves, and what we get as a result is a nation that's 90 percent Christian, yet the socioeconomic and political conditions continue to get worse. The rich get richer and the underclass expands.

Once a very cynical man approached me and asked me, "If your God is so loving and all powerful, why does he let people starve and live in the streets?" I looked at him and said, "My God doesn't let people starve and live in the streets. We do. My God does not have all the power. God made me in the image of God's self and God shares power with me. Unlike any other creature I have the power to make a choice. God in and through Christ empowers me to make a difference in my life and in this world." Oh, come, Jesus Christ, come! And come he does, for in the midst of our misunderstanding and false expectations, God loves us and gives the free gift of life in spite of us. In this season of Advent, come, Jesus Christ, come!

We must pause and ask ourselves, "What am I expecting for Christmas?" I don't know what you expect but I can tell you what you'll get. If you only let God, God will do great things in your life. No, Christ won't transform the world but he'll transform you. You'll become an agent of transformation for the Master. God in and through Christ will give the power to transform your life and your world.

What's on your Christmas list this year? Well, my friends, on Christmas day Jesus has the perfect gift for you. Let's sneak a peak and look under the tree. To our surprise there's only one gift there and it's not even wrapped. It's old, rugged, and made of wood. This may not be what you asked for but here it is: it's an old rugged cross! Wait a minute, there's a letter tied to the cross. It's not written in ink, it's written in blood and here's what it says:

"My child, pick up this cross daily and follow me. I want you to love God with all you heart, and with all your mind, and with all your soul. I want you to love your neighbor as you love yourself."

Some people might stop reading the letter by now because this is not the gift they were expecting for Christmas. This is not one of the gifts you had on your list. But if you dare to read on, the letter says: "I know you have a Christmas list. I knew about it before you wrote it, but seek ye first the kingdom of God and God's righteousness and all these things shall be yours as well.

"Go ahead and pick up my gift to you. I know it's heavy and the road you'll travel will be rough. I never promised you that it would be easy. You'll get tired but when you do, come to me, all who are heavy laden, and I will give you rest. Take my yoke upon you and learn from me, for I am gentle, and lowly in heart, and you will find rest for your souls. For my yoke is easy and my burden is light.

"You see the gift that I freely give, yet you hesitate to accept it. I realize that this gift is not what you expected for Christmas but I bid you to pray before you decide, for anyone who does not take his cross and follow me is not worthy of me. O ye of little faith, let those who have ears listen. I am the one who was with God in the beginning. I am the light that shines in darkness, and the darkness cannot overcome me. God loves you so much that God sent me not to condemn you but that you might be saved through me.

"If you decide to accept my gift, and I pray that you do, go and make disciples of all the nations, baptizing them in the name of the Father, and of the Son, and of the Holy Spirit. Teach them all that I have commanded you, and lo I am with you always, to the close of the age."

And the letter is signed, not with one name but with five:

> "Eternally yours,
>
> Wonderful Counselor,
> Mighty God,
> Everlasting Father,
> Prince of Peace,
> Jesus the Christ"

P.S. Merry Christmas!

*W*orking Out What Is Worked In

William L. Lee

William Lee is pastor of the Loudon Avenue Christian Church in Roanoke, Virginia. He is a graduate of Virginia State College and Duke University Divinity School. Bill is in great demand as a preacher, and spoke at the General Assembly of the Christian Church (Disciples of Christ) in Tulsa, Oklahoma, in 1991.

Philippians 2:12–13

Therefore, my beloved, just as you have always obeyed me, not only in my presence, but much more now in my absence, work out your own salvation with fear and trembling; for it is God who is at work in you, enabling you both to will and to work for his good pleasure.

The text before us was not written to the world. It was addressed to the church. So often we are guilty in the church of giving mail to the wrong person. A sinner, a person who knows not Jesus in the pardoning of sin, cannot do what Paul instructs us to do in this text. If there is any here who has never confessed with your mouth the Lord Jesus, and has not believed in your heart that God raised him from the dead, then you can't perform the task that Paul lays before us. If you have not been born again of the Spirit then this text was not addressed to you. You shouldn't get discouraged if you find that you are not included—stick around and I will show you how to get on the mailing list.

As I have already stated, this letter is addressed to the church. In the opening verse of the first chapter Paul defined his audience: "Paul and Timothy, servants of Christ Jesus, to all the saints...who are at Philippi, with the bishops and deacons." This letter is to all the saints at Philippi. Since God's word is eternal, we can rightly assume that what was written to Philippi was written to all of us. If that word *saint* makes you uncomfortable, let me try to define it. A saint is an earthly person who has been set apart by a divine call to do heavenly work. Saints are persons who know Jesus in the pardoning of their sin and who are walking in the newness of life by the power of the Holy Spirit. A saint is a person in the world but not of the world. A saint is an imperfect person who through the power of the Spirit is pressing and struggling toward the perfection found in Christ Jesus. A saint is a crooked person who has decided to go straight.

Paul wanted to be sure that there was no confusion as to whom this letter was written. He inserts another term to define his audience. He refers to his audience as "beloved." That's the language of the church of the Lord Jesus Christ. Paul further attempts to clarify to whom he is writing by calling them "the children of obedience." He writes that the Philippians have always obeyed. Only children of God are called obedient. Toward the end of the letter Paul calls the Philippians brethren—again the language of the church. I hope it is clear that Paul is not talking to sinners, but to the church.

Now that we have established Paul's audience, let us hear what God wants us to do.

> Therefore, my beloved, just as you have always obeyed me, not only in my presence, but much more now in my absence, work out your own salvation with fear and trembling; for it is God who is at work in you, enabling you both to will and to work for his good pleasure.
> Philippians 2:12–13

God wants us to "work out what is worked in." This text has often been misinterpreted by many in the church. Many feel that they have to do good work to earn salvation. This text does not mean this; Paul would be contradicting himself if it did. Paul wrote these words concerning the subject of salvation to the church at Ephesus:

> For by grace you have been saved through faith, and this is not your own doing; it is the gift of God—not the result of works, so that no one may boast.
> Ephesians 2:8–9

Paul writes also in Romans 3:24, "they are now justified by his grace as a gift." You can see that Paul could not possibly mean for us to earn salvation. Our salvation was purchased long ago. The old account was settled long ago. The precious blood of Jesus purchased our pardon. On a hill called Calvary, Jesus paid it all. While we were yet sinners Christ died for the ungodly. Fannie Crosby knew how our salvation was purchased:

> To God be the glory, great things he has done!
> So loved he the world that he gave us his son,
> Who yielded his life an atonement for sin
> And opened the lifegate that all may go in.

Well, if Paul is not talking about earning our salvation, what does he mean when he writes, "Work out your own salvation with fear and trembling"? I believe that Paul is saying to the saints that we must have an outward manifestation of an inward reality. That inward reality is that we have been saturated with the sacred sweets of the Spirit. That word *manifest* means to make plainly apparent, to make obvious, to reveal, to show, to display, to prove, to be evident, to give a sign or indication.

To work out our own salvation is to make it plainly apparent to those with whom we come in contact that we have Christ Jesus in us. To work out our own salvation is to make it obvious to those within and without that something has happened to us. To work out our own salvation is to reveal that we're not what we used to be. To work out our own salvation is to show that we have changed and we are still changing. To work out our own salvation is to daily display divine characteristics. To work out our own salvation is to prove to people by our living that the Lord Jesus makes a difference in your life. To work out our own salvation is to give some evidence to the court of the world that the blood never loses its power. To work out your own salvation is to give a sign, some indication that you have been born again. This is what Paul was getting at, "work out what is worked in."

Now it is safe to assume that if God has not worked something in, we can't work something out. That's why this letter is written exclusively to the church. God has put something within you and me. All the people I know that have been pricked in their hearts by the word of truth, who have repented of their sins and have been baptized, have something within them from God. The Bible is clear on this. John 1:12 declares, "But to all who received him, who believed in his name, he gave power to become children of God." Peter declares that after we repent and are baptized we shall receive the Holy Spirit. Paul declares, "But you are not in the flesh, but in the Spirit, if so be the Spirit of God dwells in you." God has put his Holy Spirit within us. He desires that we "work out what is worked in."

I am discovering in the church that we are waiting, pushing, encouraging people to produce fruit—many times to our own frustration and to their discouragement. At some point we must realize that if it is not within, it won't be manifested without. My father used to say, "You can't get blood out of a turnip." Jesus put it this way: "A good tree cannot bear bad fruit, nor can a bad tree bear good fruit" (Matthew 7:18).

On the other hand, there are people who have the Spirit within but will not work it out. We can learn a valuable lesson from the fig tree that Jesus cursed. Jesus knew that this tree should bear fruit. The Creator had put all things needed to bear fruit in this tree. In spite of all its potential this fig tree only worked out a trunk, some branches, some leaves, some flowers, but no fruit, no figs. Church people are like that. We partially work out what is worked in. Everybody will not produce the same yield but we ought to complete the yield that is within us. Jesus told us in the parable of the sower that some will yield 30, some 60, and others 100. He does not expect a person in whom he has invested a 30-yield Spirit to produce a 100-yield crop. Nor does he expect a person in whom he has invested a 100-yield Spirit to produce a 30-yield crop. Work out what has been worked in. If he put 30 in you and you work out 30 in God's eyesight you have done the same as the person who had within 100 and worked out 100.

There is a reason why many who have the Spirit find it difficult to work out what is worked in. Paul says to work out your own salvation in fear and in trembling. He did not say work out your husband's. He did not say work out your wife's. He did not say work out your neighbor's. He did not say work out all the church members'. He did not say work out the entire city's. He did not say work out the preacher's. Work out your own salvation.

Solomon will tell you what will happen if we spend our time working out what's in other people. In the Song of Solomon, he trumpets, "They made me keeper of the vineyards, but my own vineyard I have not kept!" I was so busy keeping weeds out of other people's gardens that weeds have overtaken mine. I was so busy irrigating other vineyards that mine is bone dry. I was so busy tending the vineyards that mine has gone unattended. My brothers and sisters, God has planted a vineyard in you and me. We ought to work out what the Lord has worked in. It delights God, it pleases God, when we work out what is worked in. In Galatians 5, Paul refers to us as a vineyard. The seed that produces the fruit of the Spirit was planted by God. The ground was plowed by his word and fertilized by his blood.

Love is in you—work it out!
Joy is in you—work it out!
Peace is in you—work it out!
Patience is in you—work it out!
Gentleness is in you—work it out!
Goodness is in you—work it out!
Faith is in you—work it out!
Meekness is in you—work it out!
Temperance is in you—work it out!

These are the fruits of the Spirit. God has put all of this in us. We ought to work out what has been worked in.

The world of nature is beckoning us to learn how it works out what has been worked in. Talk to a stately oak and it will tell you, "I have not always been like this. I used to be an acorn. God put everything in that acorn that I needed to be a stately oak. In that acorn was a sturdy trunk, limbs, leaves, and roots. I worked out what the Lord worked in. I became a sapling, but I was incomplete. I became a young tree, but I was not finished yet. I worked out what was worked in until I became a stately oak."

Ask the butterfly and it will tell you, "I have not always been a butterfly. I used to be a caterpillar. I used to be unattractive. God put everything in that caterpillar for me to become a butterfly. I had to go through some stages. First I was a caterpillar; then a larvae and later a cocoon. I worked out what was worked in until I became a beautiful butterfly."

Brothers and sisters, look at the rose and it will tell you that "I was a briar. God put everything in that briar for me to become a rose. It was not easy. I got snowed on so heavy that I bent under its weight. In spite of that I kept on working out. I got cut by the pruning knife, but I kept on working out. I've been dug up by my roots and have been moved from my place of origin, but I kept on working out. I've been run over by cars and bicycles, but I kept on working out. I've perspired under the heat of a noonday sun, but I've continued to work out what is worked in. Look at me now. I'm a rose. Florists get calls daily to have me arranged as an expression of love."

Like the acorn, the caterpillar, and the briar bush, God has put something within us.

> Something within me I cannot explain.
> Something within me that banishes all pain
> All I know is that there is something within.

Saints, sometimes we must work out in the midst of much tribulation. Saints, we ought to take a lesson from nature and work out what has been worked in. Yes, God has put his Spirit in us. He expects us to one day look like Jesus.

> Beloved, we are God's children now; what we will be has not yet been revealed. What we do know is this: when he is revealed, we will be like him, for we will see him as he is.
>
> 1 John 3:2

Right now we are just pencil drawings, charcoal sketches, graphics, faded snapshots, finger paintings of the image of Christ. Sin has tarnished the picture that bears the image of God. I thank God that Jesus was walking around flea markets and yard sales and saw these discarded frames and faded pictures. He took his blood and tenderly, compassionately, lovingly wiped away the tarnish of many years of sin. When the tarnish of sin was wiped away we began to work out what had been worked in. If we work diligently, tirelessly, and faithfully, we know that when he shall be revealed, we shall be like him, for we will see him as he is. No longer will we be pencil drawings. No longer will we be charcoal sketches. No longer will we be graphic drawings. No longer will we be faded snapshots. No longer will we be finger paintings. For when the blood wipes away the tarnish, we will become Rembrandts, da Vincis, Picassos and Michelangelos. We will become the portrait of Christ.

My brothers and sisters, I encourage you to work out what has been worked in.

Preachers, God has worked a sermon in you, preach it out.
Choir members, God has worked a song in you, sing it out.
Elders, God has worked a prayer in you, pray it out.
Deacons, God has worked a service in you, serve it out.
Saints, God has worked a testimony in you, talk it out.
Saints, God has holy living in you, live it out.
Saints, God has worked joy in you, shout it out.

How long must we work out what is worked in? Work, says Paul, "until all of us come to the unity of the faith and of the knowledge of the Son of God, to maturity, to the measure of the full stature of Christ" (Ephesians 4:13).

I want to be more like Jesus. I want to walk like him. I want to talk like him. I want to pray like him. I want to forgive like him. I want to love like him. Do you want to be more like Jesus? Then work out what is worked in.

I said from the outset that this letter was not mailed to sinners. I also told you that I would show you how to get on the mailing list. Paul tells us that "if you confess with your lips that Jesus is Lord and believe in your heart that God raised him from the dead, you will be saved. For one believes with the heart and so is justified, and one confesses with the mouth and so is saved" (Romans 10:9–10).

Changing Shoes

L. Wayne Stewart

Wayne Stewart serves as administrative director of
the Reconciliation program of the Church Finance
Council of the Christian Church (Disciples of Christ).
Formerly the pastor of churches in north central Texas,
his home state, Wayne has been an executive in
business. He has degrees from Prairie View A. & M.,
Northwest Christian College, and Brite Divinity School of
Texas Christian University. This sermon was delivered at
the National Convocation of the Christian Church, in
Memphis, Tennessee.

Luke 7:11–23

From this passage of scripture I want to lift out verse 22 as
my text for this evening. Jesus said to the messengers, "Go
and tell John what you have seen." I want to use as my subject
tonight "Changing Shoes." Changing shoes. And I might as
well confess up front—because you will discover this truth
before I sit down—at this point in my ministry I have not yet
mastered the two-point, three-point, four-or-more-point sermon. All I know how to do is preach a one-point sermon. So I
will be using all the revelation and inspiration that God has
given me from this text to make one point, and that one point
will be based on the premise that all of us walking around now
are walking around in shoes that will some day be passed on
to the future generations. And my point will be some of those
shoes are not worth having. "I got shoes, you got shoes, all
God's chillun got shoes." All the shoes that we are walking

51

around in today at some time in the future will be passed on to future generations. Some of those shoes ain't worth having.

Now the best example I know to illustrate this actually comes from a true story—a story that happened one time in the project. But the problem with this story is that Jesus' church is so divided, mixed up and confused about what we mean when we say *project*, till I fear that most of us will not get the meaning of the story and therefore not know the significance of these shoes that I need to talk to you about. So before we tell the story let's spend just a few moments with each other to see if we can come together with our definition of *project*.

No, a project is not that place where people choose to go to live, those folk who "ain't doing nothing, ain't never done nothing, and ain't goin' never do nothing." A project is not some place that people dream up in their minds that they can go to and get extraordinary dehumanization processes forced on them. A project is not a place where human beings go so they can hide behind the excuse, "I cain't do better." And no, a project is not really that place over yonder across the track where all of them funny-looking folk, those funny-acting, funny-walking, funny-talking, and funny-smelling folk live. But a project is a designated residential area with a selected population who live a regulated lifestyle to produce expected results.

Now, if you missed that, a project is a place where all of the decisions that control the human lives that live there are decided by folk on the outside. The truth is, all of us here really come from the project. If you don't believe that, let's see if you can pass this test. Were you the one who sent in the names to the Democratic and Republican Parties two years ago about who would be the nominees this year? No. Well, then, you live in a project. Do you know the name, age, sex, religious preference of your next state governor? You live in a project. Do you make any of the final decisions that have to do with the quality of life in your neighborhood, such as the quality of the education system or the quantity of the police officers in your neighborhood? You live in a project. And before we go any further it would be good for all of us to agree on one thing, that all of us here tonight, regardless of what you think of yourself and where you come from, everybody here has the same zip code, and it is P-R-O-J-E-C-T.

So listen up, this story I am about to tell is really your story. It happened in your town, in your neighborhood, on your street. The truth is, some of you portray the main character. I need to tell you a story about an event that happened one ordinary day in an ordinary place that we are all familiar with that we need to call tonight, "the project." Wasn't nothing extraordinary about this day; it was a typical day in the project. There had been four or five fistfights, seven or eight persons had been arrested, six families had been evicted. There had been twenty-seven color televisions on this side of the project and sold that same day on this side of the project. And ain't nothing unusual about that. And there had been a shooting. Some woman thought she overheard somebody saying that they thought they heard somebody saying that they saw somebody who looked like her husband with another woman. See, people die from no more than that in the project.

But along about five-thirty in the afternoon one of the doors to one of the upstairs apartments swung open and out stepped mister tall, dark, and handsome. One of the most notorious residents of the project, but nobody had seen him all day, but that was ordinary. You see, mister tall, dark, and handsome was what we called down home a "night owl." He spent the night hours hooting all over town and he spent the daylight hours sleeping and chilling out at his apartment. It's late in the evening now. It's time for him to get up and go check up and be sure that all of his gambling joints are opened up, all of his bootleg places filled up, his dope pushers stocked up and his prostitutes lined up, because this is Friday evening, don't you see, and he's expecting to clean up. Happens every day in the project.

When he got to the end of the stairs one of the brothers lingering in the shade of the gallow tree says, "What's happening, Jack?" And Jack wheeled as only he could do it and said, "That be Mister Big Jack to you." And then he turned and kinda threw him across the parking lot. You could just see that Aramis 600 just oozing off him as he walked, but when he bent over, when he bent over to unlock the door to his 360, the unexpected happened. A voice from an unseen person literally came out and gripped his soul. A little voice said, "What's happening, Mister Big Jack?"

Jack turned around and looked and he said, "Reverend, it literally broke my heart." It was a little black boy, about ten years old, a boy with a body that revealed in a most excellent way malnutrition. A little boy with a face that spelled abuse, who was wearing clothes that were the best example Jack had ever seen in his life of neglect. Jack said, "Reverend, he had some of those little old beady shiny eyes that looked to me like they looked up from nothing out into nowhere. And this little kid stood there grinning up at me and said, 'What's happening, Mister Big Jack? Say, Mister Big Jack, when I grow up I wanta be just like you, Mister Big Jack. I wanta get me some of them "bad rags" just like yours, Mister Big Jack, gonna drive me one of them Merceedes Beens, just like yours, Mister Big Jack. Mister Big Jack, can I have them shoes you wearing? No, I don't mean right now, Mister Big Jack, but when *you* get through walking in them, can I have your shoes, Mister Big Jack?"

You see, church, there's something to learn from this story that happens all too often in the project. Either intentionally or unintentionally, all of us here tonight are walking in shoes that at some point in time will be passed on to the future generation. And before we get to the point where we pass off blindly, maybe tonight is a good night for us to stop and check out our shoes. Because, you see, the shoes you walk around in determine the path that you walk in, and the path you walk in determines what you see, and what you see determines whether or not you will end up totally blind or receive eternal sight. You see, darkness produces darkness and the end result is total blindness. Light reflects light, and the result of that is eternal sight. Convocation of the Christian Church, Disciples of Christ in the United States and Canada, check out your shoes, because some of us here tonight are wearing shoes that ain't worth having.

The truth is we have some *prancing* shoes at the Convocation. Now I know they're here because they show up every Sunday morning at our churches. A group comes in at eleven fifteen, more at eleven twenty, some more at eleven twenty-five, and the grand entry at twenty minutes after twelve! Prancing shoes! Prance from the back door of the church all the way up to the front row. Chanting as they go: "I come from Neiman's; I come from Neiman's; I come from Neiman's. You come from K-Mart; you come from K-Mart." Prancing shoes. Now if that's all that's seen at Convocation churches no wonder there's so much blindness in our church.

We got some *dancing* shoes at Convocation. All through the week they dance all over town, in and out of one inconspicuous hotel and motel and into another one, pausing for a quickie rendezvous with other shoes that do not live in their closet. Most of the time they are shoes of the opposite sex, sometimes they are shoes of the same sex, but almost all of the time they are shoes from the same church. That kind of stuff will cause total blindness to Jesus' church.

We have some *stomping* shoes in the church. If you don't believe me you better not wake up someday and start looking around at all of this obsolescence, analyzing all of this irrelevance, checking out all of the isolation and insulation, and start talking to God about it and praying about it, and meditating about it, and then go back up to your church and open your mouth and say something that's gonna cause some changes at your church. Just about the time you get that first sentence out of your mouth that's gonna produce some relevance, some new life, a new way and a new day, them stomping shoes will get you. Now that kind of activity can produce nothing but blindness.

Jesus' church has been called by the Spirit to give sight to the blind. We're so filled with activities that produce total blindness. "Well, Mister Big Jack, what did you learn?" He said, "Well, Stewart, I learned something that I can never live with. I never knew it but everything I did, everywhere I went all of my life, there was somebody watching me and I could not stand myself any longer when this little boy asked me to allow him to stand in *my* shoes! Because if there's anything in this world that I never want to have happen, it's for any human being to have to go through this hell that I've gone through! Reverend, you got to help me because I got to have something that's gonna help this little boy because if there's ever anybody who needs help it's this little kid. And I've got to have something to pass on to him that is going to be life producing."

"Well, Jack, you know I'm a preacher, I'm not a miracle worker. All I can talk to you about is what I know. And I do remember one time there was a man named Jesus and he went to his church."

"Naw, Reverend, I don't want to talk to you about church. That's my problem: I already know too much about them church folk. You see, Reverend, the church folk think that God comes down to Tennessee every now and then to visit and that's good enough for them. So when God shows up in Tennessee they run out and say, 'God, I'm gonna serve you till I die if it don't rain.' And then they go back to doing the same old things they been doing. The last thing in the world I want to hear more about, Reverend, is them church folk."

"Yeah, Mister Big Jack, our church folks don't know that God lives in Missouri. If you tell God you love him, the next words that come out of his mouth is 'Show me.' But, Jack, you really cannot just look to flesh and blood for the answers, you can't just look at Christians, you can't just look at human beings, we have to look at a perfect model. We have to look beyond all of the frailty and mistakes and accidents and incidents that engage our lives. We have to transcend everything that is humanness and look at a perfect model. Jack, I want to talk with you just a little bit about a perfect model. A man named Jesus, who not only stood up in the midst of his people and promised to give sight to the blind, but actually went out and did it."

"Reverend, I don't believe that."

"Well, Jack, one day after John the Baptist had been locked up, he sent some of his disciples to this Jesus, and when they got to Jesus they said, 'Sir, are you the one we are looking for or should we look for another?' Now, Jack, what happened was when the people asked Jesus of Nazareth that question, he reached down and unbuckled his shoes and he stepped out of his shoes and he said to these disciples who had come with the question, 'Stand in my shoes.' You see, Jack, when you stand in his shoes there's something about the darkness there that will not allow you to look over all of this nonsense that keeps blinding us humans. But there is something about standing in Jesus' shoes. Standing in the shoes that not only came as the light but who was himself the light. It allows you to see past all of our differences and difficulties through all of our pride and prejudices and see what Almighty God wishes for his people. You see, Jack, Jesus' shoes are nothing less than shoes of faith."

It's good for us, Convocation, to learn that we can never see what God wants us to see standing in shoes for fashion, but we've got to kick off these shoes for fashion and step into our shoes of faith. It is only in shoes of faith that you can see those homeless people standing two blocks from your church starving to death. It is only when you stand where Jesus stood that you can see these little old ladies going in front of your church at eleven o'clock on Sunday morning while you're singing "O, How I Love Jesus" with five dollars in your benevolence fund. It is only when you stand where Jesus stood that you can taste poverty when you drive by. It is only when you're standing in shoes of faith, standing where Jesus stood, can you ever go out and really proclaim sight in this blind world.

But now don't anybody get excited and please don't anybody run out and jump in your shoes before you hear the rest of the story, for these are not fashion shoes. There is no design about them that you would rush out and really desire them, really. And the closer you get to them the more undesirable they become, because they have a bad smell about them. They smell like lost humanity, and when you smell them you know that these shoes have been worn by somebody who has been going out among the sick and the afflicted and the needy and the cast outs and the forced outs and the put outs. These shoes have a big hole right down through the middle of them and you don't have to be a forensic expert to figure out the hole was made with some feet in them.

You have to check out these shoes but don't go window shopping. These shoes are not for people who are casual window shoppers and you have to be careful even messing around with them, because they have some red gooey stuff on them. If you're not serious about giving sight to this blind world, don't mess around and get none of that red gooey stuff on you. Because it will not only get on you but it will get in you and when you start trying to rub it off your hand it'll get all in your hands and the first thing you know your hands will be new. And if you try to wipe it off your hands and keep on rubbing on your leg, the next thing you know your feet will be new too. And in privacy you try to wipe it off your hands and the more you work and are getting this old stony heart of yours and the first thing you know, you have a new heart.

Get it all in your mind. Change the way you think about yourself. Change the way you think about all of them folks you used to call funny-looking and funny-smelling. Change the way you think about God Almighty who created heaven and earth. And if you don't hurry up and get your hands now in some of that red stuff, it will drip down in your eyes, cause the scales of prejudice to fall off, scales of separation to fall off, scales of sexism to fall off and all of those things that divide brothers and sisters and mothers and fathers. It will be falling from your eyes and you can see clearly all of God's children who stand in need of God's grace.

Church needs to check out the shoes. Walking around in fashion shoes, fashion shoes lead to blindness. For the church of Jesus Christ to do the job Jesus has called us to do, we're gonna have to put on our shoes of faith. Then when we have finished our assignment, when we have completed the task, when we have walked our last mile, there will be no hesitation in our souls and we can say with full confidence and full assurance to all of those future generations who follow us, "Fill these shoes."

$\mathcal{D}$eep River

T. J. Bottoms

T. J. Bottoms is pastor of All Peoples Christian
Church in Los Angeles, California. A Timothy from Light
of the World Christian Church in Indianapolis, Indiana,
where he served as associate minister, T.J. has degrees
from Jarvis Christian College and the School of Theology
at Claremont. This sermon was delivered on May 1,
1994, at Central Christian Church in Indianapolis.

Psalm 46: 1–4a; Isaiah 66:12; Psalm 137:1–4

Deep river, my home is over Jordan,
Deep, deep river, Lord, I want to cross over into
    campground.
O don't you want to go to that gospel feast,
That promised land where all is peace, O....

———————

God is our refuge and strength,
    a very present help in trouble.
Therefore we will not fear, though the earth should
    change,
    though the mountains shake in the heart of the sea;
though its waters roar and foam,
    though the mountains tremble with its tumult.
There is a river whose streams make glad the city of God.
                                        Psalm 46:1–4a

59

I will extend peace to her like a river.

                                    Isaiah 66:12, KJV

By the rivers of Babylon...
    we sat down and...wept
    when we remembered Zion.
On the willows there
    we hung up our harps.
For there our captors
    asked us for songs,
and our tormentors asked for mirth, saying,
    "Sing us one of the songs of Zion!"
How could we sing the LORD's song
    in a foreign land?

                                    Psalm 137:1–4

One of my first responsibilities as a student minister, years ago, was to accompany twenty-six youth to northern Minnesota for a conference. While we were there, we found ourselves at the place where the great Mississippi River begins. It's just a tiny little stream—so small that one of the younger children was able to stand with one foot on each side of it. The mighty Mississippi River that is a mile wide by the time it reaches New Orleans, that touches thirty-one states including the Ohio and Missouri Rivers as its tributaries—the source of this mighty river that has been written about and sung about all these years is a small stream so narrow that a child can straddle it.

In my meditations with those youth, I recalled for them the first time I took a long-distance bus trip with my mother to her hometown in the South when I was about twelve. We crossed that same river. It was so wide, so expansive, and at that time it was so turbulent, that I remember a woman sitting behind us began to pray, out of her fear that we might fall in. Falling in never occurred to me until then, and the turbulence seemed insignificant till then. I suspect I started to pray too. But the real significance of these two visits to the Mississippi River had much to do with perspective and experience.

That woman's need to pray suggested an experience with the waves and vicissitudes of life of which my life had somehow been spared. But her prayer became mine. And it is precisely that sense of vicarious perspective and experience that takes us back to the African-American spirituals. It is not our experience, or even our perspective...but God's Holy Spirit somehow miraculously makes their experience and their perspective ours. We ponder and reflect and celebrate their vibrant, enthusiastic, valiant, and triumphant—singing faith. Theirs was a faith that was as lyrical as it was turbulent…and even their most mournful, sorrowful dirge hymns had coursing through their lyrics an undercurrent of praise, adoration, and expectation, and we turn to those spirituals seeking to find our own "sing'n' faith."

When the slaves sang, "Deep river, my home is over Jordan, deep, deep river, Lord, I want to cross over into campground. O don't you want to go to that gospel feast, that promised land where all is peace"—when they sang that song, they sang their faith. No hymn of preparation: when they sang, it was not out of their intellect or head, but their song emanated from their heart. Theirs was a faith that was tremendously rooted and grounded in what they had heard about Yahweh through the tattered pages of the Black preacher's Old Testament narration. They had heard that that which had brought them to captivity, that which served as their boundary, that which had kept them prisoner, was simultaneously that which could offer them redemption. It was simultaneously that which could provide them solace and ultimately that which would provide them salvation from the troubles of this world.

For every verse of "Deep River" that spoke clearly of a home not made by hands, there was a corresponding verse of another spiritual that spoke of God's redemption made available through baptism, for they also sang, "Take me to the river, take me to the river, take me to the river…to be baptized!" That which literally embodied their troubles could and ultimately would provide them with their physical and spiritual salvation. And so they sang! They sang, because they *knew* in what they believed.

They knew something of what Jacob heard when God said in Isaiah 43:1–3, "[The One] who created you,… [the One] who formed you…[says,] 'Do not fear, for I have redeemed you; I have called you by name, you are mine. When you pass through the waters, I will be with you; and through the rivers, they shall not overwhelm you.…For I am the LORD your God, the Holy One of Israel, your Savior.'" So they could sing, "I tole Jesus, it'd be all right, if he chang'd ma name!"

They had heard about Joshua's instructions at the banks of the river Jordan in Joshua 3:5 when he said, "Sanctify yourselves, for tomorrow the Lord will do wonders among you." So they could sing, "Keep your lamps trimmed and burning!"—which was a clarion call to "be ready!" And the Israelites carried the ark of the covenant across the river that had been flooded without ever even getting the hems of their garments wet. They heard the story of Joshua 4:18 about how the priests came up out of the river carrying the ark of the covenant of the Lord. And no sooner had they set their feet on dry ground, the Jordan River returned to its flood stage. They heard from Joshua in chapter 24 when he said God called them to remember the God who had delivered them out of the hands of the captor. So they sang "Joshua fit' the battle of Jericho!" And they learned to say like the psalmist in Psalm 46: "God is our refuge and strength, a very present help in trouble. Therefore we will not fear, though the earth should change, though the mountains shake in the heart of the sea; though its waters roar and foam, though the mountains tremble with its tumult."

There is another river....There is a river, whose streams make glad the city of God. So they could proclaim, "The Lord Almighty is with us; the God of Jacob is our fortress. Come and see the works of the Lord, the desolations he has brought on the earth. He makes wars to cease to the ends of the earth. He breaks the bow and shatters the spear, he burns the spear with fire, be still and know that I am God; I will be exalted among the nations, I will be exalted in the earth. The Lord Almighty is with us; the God of Jacob is our fortress. And as they rehearsed what God had done in the lives of God's people, they couldn't help but to wonder, "Don't you wanna go?"

The slaves could sing in the midst of their adversity because their faith was seeped and sinewed in the knowledge that their God—the God of Abraham, Isaac, and Jacob—Jehovah, the Rose of Sharon, the Lily of the Valley, the Bright and Morning Star, the Great "I Am," the Wheel in the Middle of the Wheel, the Unmoved Mover, the very Creator of the ends of the earth, was not somehow distant from them, or aloof to their travail...but that miraculously, though they could not articulate it, their transcendent God of the cosmos was also imminent, present, intimate, and familiar with them in the midst of their adversity; as near as their very breathing and acquainted with their grief. So they could proclaim with those who preceded them, "By the rivers of Babylon, we sat and wept when we remembered Zion. On the willows there we hung up our harps. For there our captors asked us for songs, and our tormentors asked for mirth, saying, 'Sing us one of the songs of Zion!' How could we sing the LORD'S song in a foreign land?"

Though they cried, they never claimed to cry alone. They knew that God was grieving with them. They knew something about captivity, and they knew that captivity wasn't their home. They believed that their God would deliver their freedom. Theirs was a *deep-river-and-strange-land faith!* Victory and salvation were within sight in their mind's eye...but there were depths that they could not cross alone and often their only recourse was to sing in the midst of their tears.

Your pastor says it beautifully in her contribution to the book *Conservative, Moderate, Liberal,* when she writes, "One weeps when one's freedom to change the situation is limited....We weep...because finally, whatever we do does not undo what is history. In short, we weep at tragedy." The slaves wept and simultaneously sang when they considered the river, for it represented their boundary beyond which they could not go...and it simultaneously represented the very possibility of the "crossin' ovah!" or their salvation! They knew that God's plan was for them to reach the "promis'd land"...and since it was God's plan, they knew that God would surely show them the way and the rivers and strange lands were merely part of the journey! But until that time, they had to sing—sing in order to keep from crying, and sing while crying, sing in order to continue to tell the story in a way that they could communicate even while the master was standin' over them, sing in order for their children to hear that "weeping endureth for a night but joy cometh in the morning."

So they could say with great resolve, "Soon Ah will be done-a with the troubles of this world, the troubles of this world, the troubles of this world." They sang in that strange land because they knew that a new day was coming and they could shout about it with the lyrics "In that great gittin' up morning!!! Fare thee well, Fare thee well!"

It was Maya Angelou who wrote almost one hundred years later in *I Know Why the Caged Bird Sings,* "The slaves knew that slavery was not their final destination and that captivity was but for a moment." And the joy of "crossin' ovah" would more than compensate for hardships they would endure. So you can hear them proclaim, "Wouldn't take nothin' for the journey!"

I can only imagine their experience. But Wednesday, as I watched the dismantling of apartheid with the first multi-racial election in South Africa's history, I understood perhaps for the first time in my thirty-four years the tears and the celebration. We pray God's blessings upon all the people of South Africa as they make this mammoth step—for the Whites whose lives are now faced with the most dramatic change we could imagine, and for the Blacks who will for the first time experience the challenge of being responsible for their own destiny. May God bless them all as they embark on this journey through the turbulent waters visited by this country only a few decades ago. This, like every biblical account of "crossin' ovah," requires a radical "Deep River/Strange Land" faith that refuses to accept that this life is all there is.

You and I are called to have that same faith. In the midst of the deep rivers of our lived experience, whatever your river looks like—be it cancer, AIDS, loneliness, despair, depression, oppression, or anger—you and I are compelled to call up our collective memories of how God has triumphantly acted in human history. Cancer may not seem like a deep river, but it is if you or a loved one is going through it. But it is a river over which God has carried many a thousand! AIDS may not seem like a deep river but it is if you are expected to keep it to yourself. But even this is a river to which our God is able to speak peace. Loneliness may not seem so deep to you, but if you've never been all alone down here, you just don't know what a deep-river loneliness can be. Yes, it is true, that the slaves could identify with the children of Israel, and so they could identify ways that God would surely bring them out just as God did before.

You and I, too, must come to the place where we can see that we are traveling through a strange land and our faith and our God calls us to sing in the midst of these strange lands. We must sing in the face of drugs, we must sing in the face of racism, sexism and homophobia, crime and hatred. We must sing about a God who is as near as our breathing and capable of hearing even our faintest cry. We must sing so that those who are listening might come to know that "up above our heads there's a God somewhere!"

You know something about "Deep Rivers" and "Strange Lands." But you need to take courage from yet another African-American spiritual and begin to sing, "Good news! Chariot's a comin'!" And just like those slaves who preceded us in the faith, someone will ask how is it that you can face the rivers of your existence, how is it you can endure hardship, loneliness, sickness, and despair, and sing. You can proclaim, "I sing because I'm happy, I sing because I'm free, God's eye is on the sparrow....so I know She watches me." Maybe you don't know enough of the spirituals to borrow their song. Then sing your own song, but by all means sing.

How firm a foundation, ye saints of the Lord,
is laid for your faith in God's excellent word!
What more can She say than to you She hath said,
to you who for refuge to Jesus have fled?

"Fear not, I am with thee, O be not dismayed,
for I am thy God, and will still give thee aid;
I'll strengthen thee, help thee, and cause thee to stand,
upheld by my righteous, omnipotent hand.

"When through the deep waters, I call thee to go,
the rivers of sorrow shall not overflow;
for I will be with thee thy troubles to bless,
and sanctify to thee thy deepest distress.

"When through fiery trials thy pathway shall lie,
my grace all sufficient, shall be thy supply;
the flame shall not hurt thee, I only design
thy dross to consume, and thy gold to refine.

"The soul that on Jesus still leans for repose,
I will not, I will not desert to its foes;
that soul though all hell should endeavor to shake,
I'll never, no never, no never forsake!"

———————————

Deep river, my home is over Jordan,
Deep, deep river, Lord, I want to cross over into
    campground.
O don't you want to go to that gospel feast,
That promised land where all is peace, O....

Like those who have preceded us in the faith, we too are called to traverse waters that are too deep for us alone. And we are called to walk by faith through lands that are unfamiliar to us. But we have cause to celebrate! For God truly is an ever-present help in times of trouble and the infinite Creator of the ends of the earth is there with us to guide the way. Don't you wanna go. Don't you wanna go?

*J*esus, the Resurrector

Magdalen Shelton

Magdalen Shelton is pastor of St. Phillip's Christian Church in Brooklyn, New York. A graduate of Jarvis Christian College, Magdalen has preached at many national gatherings.

John 11

We find in the eleventh chapter of John one of the most powerful stories in the New Testament, a story that reveals the awesome truth that Jesus is a resurrector. It is a story of love, commitment, power, and commission.

The scriptures teach us that a man named Lazarus became ill. His sisters, Mary and Martha, became concerned about his illness, and so they sent a message to Jesus. The message was a very simple statement. "Lord, he whom you love is ill." There was no elaboration here, no long explanation, no extensive listing of the rationale as to why Jesus should come, no expansive reminder of the family's confidence and trust in Jesus. They didn't even voice the request for him to come. Mary and Martha felt that nothing else was necessary; after all, Jesus was their good friend. They loved the Lord and he loved them. They enjoyed a special relationship

66

with the Lord. Jesus had shown so much compassion for
people he did not know, Mary and Martha just knew that
Jesus' compassion would make it necessary for him to come
and see about his friend he loved. So it was with great expectation that the sisters sent this message.

In my mind's eye I can see these sisters going out to the
road day after day, hour after hour, peering into the distance
searching for that familiar form to come into view. And I
would suppose they became more and more anxious and an-
noyed that he had not yet appeared. Can you imagine the
shock, disappointment, and perhaps even anger they must
have felt when their brother died? This should not have happened to a friend of the Master!

I'm sure that when Jesus finally arrived in Bethany, it
was with an accusing tone that the sisters said to him, "Lord,
if you had *been* here, [our] brother would not have died." In
other words, his death is on your head.

They believed that Jesus' presence could have extended
their brother's life. After all, they knew his history. He cleansed
lepers, made the lame walk, the dumb talk, gave sight to the
blind, made the infirm whole, and calmed a raging sea. But
what they failed to understand is that in Jesus there is also
renewed or resurrected life.

Jesus told Martha that her brother would live again, and
she said, "Sure—in that great getting up morning!" Then
Jesus began to test the limits of her faith. "I am the resurrection and the life. Those who believe in me, even though they
die, will live, and everyone who lives and believes in me will
never die. Do you believe this?" Notice how Martha never
quite answers the question. Martha's faith needs to be
stretched.

Many of us believe that in Jesus there is life. We just don't
quite believe in the process of renewal. We speak about and
often hold revivals in our churches for renewed spiritual life.
But do we apply this same principle of renewal to our every-
day lives and circumstances?

Jesus said, "Take away the stone." Martha, still not fully
comprehending, protested, "No, Lord! By now he's stinking
because he is dead indeed. He's past hope, there is no chance
for renewal, just pay your respects and go home!"

Marvelous Jesus! How patient he was with Martha's un-
belief and shallow understanding, and he began to stretch her

faith. He simply said to her, "Did I not tell you that if you believed, you would see the glory of God?"

The stone was rolled away, this mighty Jesus prayed, stepped up to the silent sepulchre, and simply said, "Lazarus, come out!" One simple command and the chains of death gave up their prey as Jesus liberated Lazarus from the grip of the grim reaper. When Lazarus came forth Jesus said, "Unbind him, and let him go." Lazarus was to go forth as a living example of the power of Jesus.

But wait a minute, where can we Christians today find ourselves in this story? Surely we, like this family, claim a special relationship with the Lord. If the Lord helps anyone, surely he ought to help the Christian! And I believe there are times in the life of each and every Christian when that help is desperately needed. There are times when areas in our lives are being threatened with death itself. We cry out, "Lord, I'm sick, I'm tired, I'm weary, I'm heavy laden, I'm beaten down." We, whom the Lord loves, send out a message, "Lord, come see about me! Fix it, Lord! Save me, Lord!" But sometimes there is no immediate figure on the road to our circumstances, and after a while death takes hold.

"What kind of death do you mean, Reverend Shelton?" I hear someone asking. Sometimes hope dies. Sometimes joy dies. Sometimes trust dies. Sometimes faith dies. Sometimes peace dies. Sometimes our situations are so bad they are offensive to our senses just as surely as Lazarus' body was to those standing around his tomb.

Some of us right now might be looking at our marriages and have asked Jesus to come by before their marriages die. Things have gotten so bad that you feel there is no hope. *Jesus is a resurrector!* He is speaking to your heart, saying, "Roll away the stone"—the stone of pride, the stone that won't allow you to say I'm sorry, the stone that blocks forgiveness, the stone that rules out compromise and communication. Roll away the stone and I will call forth new life!

Some of us might be having trouble with our children and think the relationship is dead, but Jesus says, "Roll away the stone"—the stone of stubbornness, the stone of harshness, the stone of indifference, the stone of anger, the stone of hurt. Roll away the stone and I will give new life.

Some of us have worked hard in our lives, but we somehow feel that our work has produced no fruit. Perhaps we feel as if our effectiveness has come to an end. We might feel that in all our trying, the message of God's love we try to share never penetrates the minds and souls of anyone. Our witness has died, but Jesus is speaking! Can you hear his voice? He is saying, "Roll away the stone"—the stone of doubt, the stone of fear, the stone of inferiority, the stone of independence (as if it is on your power alone that you stand). Roll it away and I will resurrect your witness.

I can hear someone saying, "Sometimes a situation is dead and God calls for you to move on." Yes, that is true. But sometimes God also calls on us to call on his presence and power and ask him to breathe new life. Sometimes death remains where new life should be because we don't believe enough in the power of the resurrection.

Once there were two political prisoners held in separate cells down in the deepest darkest dungeon of the jail. Their only contact with the outside world was the guard who brought them their food and spat out curses and verbal abuse.

Finally, liberation came to this tiny nation. Soldiers flooded the jails, opening cells and setting the prisoners free. Someone remembered that there were prisoners locked on the lower level. They found the keys, unlocked the doors, and shouted into the darkness, "Come out, you have been set free!" One of those prisoners came out incredulously looking around and thanking God for this day long dreamed of. In great celebration and confusion they left the prison grounds. A few weeks later this prisoner was interviewed by the press. He was asked how it felt to finally be free. Then he was asked how his fellow sufferer felt about freedom. His reply was, "I haven't seen him." After a few moments it became apparent that no one had seen him. A group of solders were dispatched back to the prison. There in the far corner of the cell they found the other prisoner. He had starved nearly to death and was just breathing out his last as he explained, "I heard people shouting, you're free, but I just couldn't believe that after all this time freedom could really come. So I didn't try to open the door."

What am I trying to say? Don't miss your resurrection because you fail to believe.

Jesus says to us, "Come forth and take off these clothes that bind you, that restrict you and prevent you from doing my will." Lord, what must I loose that binds me?

Take off complacency—see no evil, hear no evil, speak no evil—I thought everything was fine—all I needed was to think good thoughts because I saw no sin. Jesus says loose yourself from complacency.

Loose yourself from negative compromise—if I talk about Jesus they might not want to be around me anymore—if I don't lie on the application I might not get the job—I'll tell the people what they want to hear and they'll call me back. Loose yourself from compromise!

Loose yourself from mediocrity—they'll accept anything, I don't have to present my best—I don't have time to study, I'll get by—no one cares if I don't do my best, besides, who will know? Jesus says loose yourself from mediocrity.

Some of you are so blessed. You have no dead areas in your lives. You have full lives in every aspect of your existence. For this you should really thank God and give him the glory. You are living proof of the abundant life in Christ. Go forth and help your sisters and brothers who need the power of Jesus, the resurrector in their lives.

But I must confess that there are areas in my life that have needed resurrection. I needed some renewal, some reviving, but I called on the Lord, "Jesus, Jesus, Jesus, Master, my Lord and my God, breathe on me for I know that you are a resurrector!" And Jesus came forth and brought new life!

Now I can sing that my hope is built on nothing less, and I will trust in the Lord because Jesus is the center of my joy, because he is the resurrector!

$\mathcal{B}$enbow Family Reunion

John Compton

John Compton has been one of the most influential ministers and leaders in the Christian Church (Disciples of Christ). He has pastored several churches, served as an associate regional minister in Ohio, regional minister in Indiana, and president of the Division of Homeland Ministries, among other responsibilities. John is a graduate of Jarvis Christian College and Christian Theological Seminary. This message was delivered at the Benbow family reunion in the Chicago area on July 11, 1993.

2 Timothy 1:1–5*

To the Benbow family officers, the Chicago-Gary host committee, relatives, friends, and attendees at this 1993 Benbow family reunion: I am pleased to have been in attendance and now to be privileged to deliver the sermon as this gathering of the clan draws to a close.

Paul, an apostle of Jesus Christ by the will of God, according to the promise of life which is in Christ Jesus, to Timothy, my dearly beloved son: Grace, mercy and peace, from God the Father and Christ Jesus our Lord. I thank God, whom I serve from my forefathers with pure conscience, that without ceasing I have remembrance of thee in my prayers night and day; greatly

---

*The scripture references in this sermon are from the King James Version of the Bible.

71

desiring to see thee, being mindful of thy tears, that I
may be filled with joy; when I call to remembrance the
unfeigned faith that is in thee, which dwelt first in thy
grandmother Lois, and thy mother Eunice; and I am
persuaded that in thee also.

As blood relations we gathered in this metroplex three
days ago to fellowship, have fun, to get to know each other, to
pray together, play together, learn from each other, to worship as family.

The glue mixed at these reunions keeps us solid and strong
as we struggle and stroll through our lives. Our kinship becomes richer. Too many families gather only for funerals or as
stopovers on the road to somewhere else. Too many families
share only greeting cards or an occasional convenient telephone conversation.

But this family are friends. There is a genuine feeling of
friendliness. Our closeness is fostered not only by blood bond
but by the friendship fueled by these reunions.

This legacy, Benbow family reunion, has been given to us—
it is important that we keep the torch burning and pass it on.

Today, with the decay of the family unit, it is very important
for us, our children, and grandchildren to know our roots. We
need to be able to identify as a family—who we are—what we
are—and with the mobility of Americans today—where we are.

The call is out for strengthening the Black family. This we
must do, for the Black family is in a perilous state today.
Studies show the family unit (the traditional family unit) as
we categorize it—father, mother, and children—is disintegrating.

Two-parent families are now in a minority. Single-parent
households, mostly headed by females, more than doubled
between 1940-1980. Additionally, 43 percent of all Black families were headed by female single parents and 52 percent of
Black children under the age of eighteen were being raised by
a single parent by the year 1984.

Also plaguing the African-American family are a myriad of
social issues—unemployment and joblessness, poverty, drug
abuse, crime, out-of-wedlock births, teenage pregnancy, quality education, and the list goes on and on.

Approximately one in four young Black males in America
is behind bars, on parole, or on probation; 23 percent of Black

men 20-29 are under the watchful eye of the criminal justice system.

The Black family is in trouble and needs to be strengthened. In every parent's week there are 168 hours: 40 hours at work; 15 hours overtime, lunch and commuting to work; 56 hours for sleep; 57 hours to spend elsewhere. How many are actually spent with the family?

If the children of today are the leaders of tomorrow then we must teach children Christian principles from day to day. Proverbs 22:6 says, "Train up a child in the way he/she should go: and when she/he is old, he/she will not depart from it."

Our ancestors left us a spiritual legacy. They embraced the teachings of the Bible, the teaching of Jesus, and passed these teachings on to their children, grandchildren, and family members.

In 2 Kings 2, Elijah's life and spiritual legacy were so impressive to Elisha that he wanted not only to inherit Elijah's spirit but wanted twice as much of it. As Elijah was about to leave the world, he asked Elisha what he could do for him before he was taken from him, and Elisha said, "[I pray you] let me inherit a double share of your spirit" (NRSV).

What a flattering request for Elijah that someone close enough to know him well would want to be not only like him, but doubly so. Elisha's ministry to Israel lasted fifty years. During this time he played a decisive part in shaping the events of that time. It seemed Elisha received a double share of Elijah's spirit.

It would appear that the Benbow descendants received a share of the sister's spirit which was rooted in the legacy of Christ. From their spiritual legacy, the Benbow family has produced good citizens, active church members—church lay leaders—deacons—elders—ministers—God-fearing and God-loving people.

In the text for the morning, 2 Timothy 1:1–5, the apostle Paul commends Timothy not simply for his faith, but for the fact that he recognized it as having been transmitted through his mother, Eunice, and his grandmother, Lois. We sometimes regard faith as a matter of personal preference and individual understanding. In contrast, Paul appeals to a genealogy for the roots of faith, heralding Timothy as its most recent branch and blossom.

When a little girl was asked why she believed in God, she paused and said, "I don't know, but I think it runs in the family." The girl probably spoke more truth than she realized. Of course, no one will go to heaven on the faith of parents or grandparents. Each must receive Christ as his or her own Redeemer. I like the answer the girl gave. She believed in Christ as her Savior, not because she had worked through intellectual difficulties. She was confident about God because "it runs in the family."

There are some things we cannot borrow. There was a man who died and went to St. Peter. He stood by the big book into which St. Peter read the names of the elect. St. Peter said to him, "We're glad to have you here. How is your relationship with the Lord?" The man said, "My father was a minister." St. Peter said, "No, your relationship?" "Well, my wife prayed daily for us and read her Bible each night." "No, your relationship?" and gradually the point was driven home. We can't borrow our family's faith; we must build our own.

Former Health and Human Services Secretary Louis Sullivan has said: "We must transform a culture of violence, which defeats and destroys, into a culture of character, which uplifts and empowers. The first step in reinvigorating a culture of character is for each and every one of us to take personal responsibility for our own lives and our health. To dwell on the belief that we are victims of someone's else's behavior—however true that may be, implies that we are powerless to make our lives better."

Sullivan quoted the late Benjamin Mays, former President of Morehouse College: "It is not your environment, it is you— the quality of your mind, the integrity of your soul, and the determination of your will that will decide your future and shape your life."

The Black family cries out to be strengthened. We can begin by strengthening our own families and family ties. What kind of legacy will you be leaving behind?

$\mathcal{R}$ise Up, O Man of God

T. Garrott Benjamin, Jr.

Thomas Garrott Benjamin has been for many years
the senior pastor of Light of the World Christian Church
in Indianapolis, one of the largest Disciples
congregations in the world. T. Garrott has preached
widely on radio and television, and currently has a
weekly television program, "Living for the City." He has
authored a book that addresses the problems of young
Black males in America, entitled *Boys to Men:
A Handbook for Survival*.

Exodus 17:8–12*

Then came Amalek, and fought with Israel in Rephidim.
And Moses said unto Joshua, Choose us out men, and
go out, fight with Amalek: tomorrow I will stand on the
top of the hill with the rod of God in mine hand. So
Joshua did as Moses had said to him, and fought with
Amalek: and Moses, Aaron, and Hur went up to the top
of the hill. And it came to pass, when Moses held up his
hand, that Israel prevailed....But Moses' hands were
heavy; and they took a stone, and put it under him, and
he sat thereon; and Aaron and Hur stayed up his hands,
the one on the one side, and the other on the other side;

---

*The scripture references in this sermon are from the King James
Version of the Bible.

75

and his hands were steady until the going down of the sun.

This is one of the most powerful stories in all of scripture. It is a story about a man who, while strong, was not strong enough. Although he was a leader, he still had feet of clay and arms that were weak—so weak that he needed the assistance of his friends to hold up his hands. It is also a story about tenacity, about staying with the goods, and about not quitting, because the scripture says that Moses' friends kept his hand steady "until the going down of the sun." This enormously powerful passage gives us a divine insight into what can happen in *our day* when men of God rise up, admit their weaknesses, and pay attention to the needs of those around them who are lacking in strength, sustenance, and stamina. While this passage from God's word is most certainly *for* women, because truth is indivisible, we must recognize that it is not *about* women. This passage calls for *men* to rise up, to stand up, and to be counted. We will therefore proceed with the interpretation of this passage and its vital importance to us today in that light.

Real Men

Wanted: Men! Real men. Men of God who have their values and their hearts in the right place. This is what our sisters want, and this is what our world demands. Now is the time to help our men become the individuals God designed them to be, and it must be done while it is still day. The plight of our people, the condition of our churches, and the direction of our nation depend on whether our men will rise up and receive their inheritance, or sit down with slumped shoulders and beg for pennies. The future of our families and the salvation of our children depend upon our men's enthusiastic response to this challenge.

For the Afrikan-American male the battle has been judged, and whether we like it or not, the jury is in and it has declared that we are *not* winning the battle. We are not even winning the skirmishes that lead to the battle. In his landmark book *Black Men: Obsolete, Single, Dangerous?* Haki R. Madhubuti reminds us that it is not a pretty sight for our brothers in American society today. Too many of our best and brightest are off the scene, doing time, doing drugs, and doing wrong. It is a sad and bitter truth that the world has gotten worse for Black men, not better. A young Black, according to the U.S. Census Bureau, has a 1 in 21 chance of being murdered, compared to 1 in 333 for a white man of the same age. This is wrong, and unless we encourage our men to rise up, where will we end up as a race? How will we tap our great inner resources and share them with the rest of the nation? Unless our men get serious about living and loving instead of lusting and leaving, we will never be able to extricate ourselves from our unacceptable predicament.

To be sure, our nation as a whole has all manner of ills, and we could spend pages quoting statistics, producing graphs, and citing experts about our *generic* problems. However, Black men in America have some specific pathologies that also need serious attention and solid solutions. It seems as if we in gospel work have too long been afraid to speak the truth about our problems. Our churches have played *possum* too long in their reticence to speak the truth in love. We all know what is going on; we simply have not had the intestinal fortitude to admit it. So let us no longer leave the solutions to secular sociologists, psychologists, and psychiatrists, as important as their contributions may be. Let us instead take the immutable, uncompromising word of God and make it our authority for understanding the issues and for coming up with solutions that reflect their eternal consequences.

But first, we must banish fear from our hearts. The apostle Paul, in 2 Timothy 1:7, wrote to Timothy, his son in the faith, that *"God hath not given us the spirit of fear, but of power, and of love, and of a sound mind."* We must help Afrikan-American men understand that they *do* have power. They *do* have love. They *do* have a sound mind. But we must be as Aaron and Hur, and step forward and hold up their hands. That man must see when his hands are raised to the glory of God—with the help of his brothers—that the enemy begins to falter. Black men must live out the experience of not only receiving help *but being willing to receive that help* from people who care about them.

Sitting Worthy at the Table

The Spirit of God is also showing us that the Afrikan-American male will never sit at the table with other worthy men until he has developed the wisdom, experience, and wherewithal to bring something *to* the table. The Black man must be built up.

He must be strong in the Lord. Our men will never even be invited to compete on a level playing field until we help them lift up their hands...until we help them build up their manhood...until we help them feel good about themselves by increasing their self-esteem. The world still sees in too many of our men only athletes and entertainers. What a limited view of our unlimited potential. Yes, we are good at these things. It is a gift enhanced by hard work. But Black men are so much more than trumpet players and point guards. We know how to think, and with the right training and direction, we also know how to act. We are men, and we are men of God!

There is one major problem, however. Every moment we delay in holding up the hands of our Afrikan-American males, it is one more moment of delay we cannot afford. Time is not on our side. The sands of time are running fast through the hourglass of opportunity, and all of us are hurting. Black boys are in trouble. Black men are in trouble. The Black family is in trouble. The Black male population in our prisons nationwide exceeds 50 percent, whereas our population in this country is only 13 percent. Of the six leading causes of death among the adult American population, Afrikan-American men head the list in every category: homicide, heart attacks, cancer, suicide, strokes, and accidents. Black men have the dubious reputation of being number one in each category. Even more frightening is the fact that Black male unemployment in this country has led to the most serious plight of our people since slavery.

Women Raising Boys

The news is not good news for Black men in the land of the free and home of the brave. Fewer than ever are free; and many are wondering if they will ever be able to brave the storms that batter them in their attempts to make something of their lives. This is the first generation where our children are killing our children. We have abandoned our responsibility for leadership in the family, in our schools, and in the church. What has been the result? For instant answers, watch CNN tonight. Read the headlines in tomorrow's paper. Pay a visit to your local police precinct late some Saturday night and ask the officer on duty how things are going. Page through your copies of *Time* and *Newsweek* or any of your favorite magazines. What do you hear, what do you see, what do you read, and what do you feel? It is not upbeat. It is not positive. It is mayhem, and our nation is coming apart at the seams.

To exacerbate the problem, our women have still been saddled with the responsibility of raising our boys. They have little choice since so many Black fathers have removed themselves from the home, and in so doing have abdicated their responsibility as husband, as father, and as friend to their children. Is there hope? Is there a way to turn it all around? Yes, praise God, there is hope, but not unless we shout the clarion cry RISE UP, O MAN OF GOD! Let us learn the lessons of biblical and secular history that hope fails and comes to no avail unless things are done in God's way, not our way. One of those ways is to remember that God's design for a father is to *need* a boy, and a boy to *need* a father. We need to give single parents high marks for doing what they are doing under what are tremendous odds. But they should not be doing the job alone. The struggles and frustrations are enormous. The bills pile up, the gangs abound, there's not enough money and hope does get thin.

That's why the man must learn to stay at home and study the art of being a father and learn the patience and love that is required in becoming a husband. When they leave the nest, fathers leave disaster in their wake. A potential model for their little Black boys is gone—sometimes forever. We need to stay with our spouses. We need to stay with our children. We need to stay with our responsibilities, and we need to stay with the church.

The sad thing is that tens of thousands of Black men have lost their focus if they are even in the picture at all. And we must say it again: our women are raising our boys all alone. But that's not all. Those same boys are impregnating girls who are having boys who are impregnating girls who are having boys who are impregnating girls who are having boys who, after having the boys, *leave home to do what they want to do.* Then, when they have moved through that confusing set of circumstances, our boys receive the final, crushing blow when they realize they must either raise themselves, or be raised by a woman—alone.

It is not in God's order of things for our women to do all the work, but praise God they are there when the man has departed. We would be in even worse shape were it not for our saintly mothers and grandmothers who have stayed with our children and come to our rescue. But it is not their sole responsibility to do it all. Our Black men have let us down—up *until now*. Some of us are working at this thing with passion and compassion. We are doing our best to make a difference.

Not long ago a young eighteen-year-old Black boy/man was asked about the direction for his life. I asked, "Son, do you have a baby?" He answered, "Yeah, I've got a little boy." "Where is your child?" "With his mother," he said.

With his mother! That is not a good answer. It is not the *correct answer*. That young man needs to be there with his wife, holding her, caressing her, comforting her, and providing for her as *together* they show their child the way.

Is There a Man in the House?

Yes, Afrikan-American males do their best with the limited resources they have been provided, and given the environment in which most have been forced to live. But the shame of it all is that so many of our Black boys grow up *never knowing their potential for good*. They don't know they can compete because they have never *believed in their heart that they have the ability to compete*. Their mothers can't teach them everything. That's why fathers must be there when it counts. Too many of our little Black boys grow up without a single model of male excellence in their lives. What happens in the light of this tragedy? Instead of producing men who are strong, energetic, kind, compassionate, and goal-oriented, we turn out little girls who have a not-so-subtle bent toward making an arbitrary choice as to their sexual preference. Read any report at the federal, state, or local level and you will discover that homosexuality is on the rise. It is proliferating on our streets, in our television shows and films, in our schools, and in our clubs. Choose virtually any location, and the gay agenda will be evident in full force.

So the question to all of us is: Do we want to do something about our dilemma? Or will we be content to sit in our rockers, wringing our hands in polite but silent disgust? If we are concerned, we must first do an inspection of our Afrikan-American homes. Is there a man on the scene? Is there a positive Black male role model present and available? Imagine the scene. It is judgment day, and the Father begins to ask row after row of men what may well be a series of very embarrassing questions, such as, "Sir, please tell me if you were there for your little boy when he needed you most?" "Did you put your hand in his hand and show him the way?" "Did you take him to church, or did you *send* him to church?" Or did you, perhaps, leave his instruction to the dope man, the bartender, or the pimp who plied his trade down an alley of sin and despair? Did you *rise up* and become the man I created you to be? What will it be like to face the Master and be obliged to tell him the truth?

Double Duty for Mother

For Black husbands and fathers, the weather is often so rough at home that they look for other ships to carry them into what they hope will be a quieter, less conflictive harbor. But God told the man at the marriage altar that he was to stay in his boat whether the sea was stormy or calm, the weather rough or smooth, the ship strong or frail. The word parents has an "s" on the end of it. The word "couple" means "two." But in the absence of Black male leadership, too many of our sisters find themselves doing double duty. They captain the ship, clean the deck, serve the mess, and clean up the mess while all the time doing their best to care for their precious cargo—their little Black boys who are learning the art of seamanship without the strong rudder of a daddy to hold their hand and show them the ropes. This is not right. A Black father must see, understand, and feel the joys of taking his rightful position as *captain* of the needs of his family. He must want to be a provider, a protector, and a priest. Above all, he must *be present.*

Not a Battle of Flesh and Blood

AIDS, Black-on-Black crime, and a proliferation of drugs and drug abuse are conquering our communities while the Black man turns his God-given power and authority over to the government, the courts, and the police. Enough is enough! The pain is too great. Our nation is tottering on the edge of disaster, and it will not get better until *we* get better—better at doing the will of God for our lives. This is no ordinary battle in which we are engaged. We are at war, and it is not a street brawl where the combatants wield guns, knives, and chains. In the words of Ephesians 6:12, we read what is still at issue today: "For we wrestle not against flesh and blood, but against principalities, against powers, against the rulers of the darkness of this world, against spiritual wickedness in high places." This is our battle, and to pretend it is anything else is to engage in delusions of unreality. That is why we must *put on the whole armor of God, that we may be able to stand against the wiles of the devil.* Unless this is our protection, we live unprotected. Unless we know who the enemy *really is,* we will never be able to defend ourselves when the going gets tough.

Nobody said this would be easy. No battle is easy. Battles are messy, bloody, difficult, and painful. If they were easy, we would call them parties, get-togethers, an afternoon in the park, or a couple of good seats on the fifty-yard line. This is war, and our men are in a state of depression, suppression, and satanic oppression. Evil spirits abound. Satan is having a field day at their expense.

Afrikan-American males are being challenged on every hand and they are not meeting the challenge. All the more reason to keep shouting *"Rise Up, O Man of God."* We need to choose some men who will help their brothers hold up their hands. We need to choose some men who will say, *"I'm ready, sign me up for the Christian Jubilee."* We need to find men who will say, *"Yes, Lord, choose me. I am tired of defeat, I want to get some victory in my life."*

In our euphoria of wanting to do the right thing, however, we must never underestimate the power of the enemy. The devil does not have the final victory, but he is a formidable adversary. Satan's plan is clear and unambiguous. He wants to destroy every Afrikan-American home, every Black man and every Black boy. He is also intent on destroying the already tenuous relationship that exists between the races, and here is how he is doing it. He develops such weak Black men that at the table of brotherhood they hardly feel worthy of showing up. Their inferiority complexes abound on the job, and they take their plummeting self-esteems with them to every other area of their lives. You cannot have brotherhood until you have two strong men who can sit at the same table, look each other in the eye, and say, *"OK brother, let's share the pie. This part belongs to me, and that part belongs to you."* But when we invite a wimp to sit alongside a man of strength, the weakling does not stand a chance. If you put a whale with a minnow, they will not enjoy much fellowship. That may not be in the Bible but it is the gospel truth. The whale will have the minnow for breakfast, lunch, and dinner. But if you put two whales across the table from each other, all they can do is look at each other and pray.

Not Alone

The message of 2 Corinthians 10:3–5 reminds us: "For though we walk in the flesh, we do not war after the flesh: (For the weapons of our warfare are not carnal, but mighty through God to the pulling down of strong holds;) Casting down imaginations, and every high thing that exalteth itself against the knowledge of God, and bringing into captivity every thought to the obedience of Christ." This is what real men—God's anointed men—must do and become. Doing it God's way will change the way we live; it will change the way we give; it will change the way we talk, and it will change the way we walk.

Now is the time to rise up, O man of God. It is time to scatter the demons of spousal abuse and parental neglect. It is time, as it was for Moses, to get someone to help hold our hands up to God. The enemy trembles when the hands of a man of God are lifted up. The enemy becomes hesitant when the hands of a man of God are lifted up. The enemy wishes he were fighting in a different zip code when the hands of a man of God are lifted up. When the battle is raging and demons and devils are everywhere, it is time for our men to raise up their hands in prayer. And if their hands are weak, we who can help must come alongside and give them a helping hand. That is what brotherhood is all about. And when we recognize that we are indeed brothers, we will know once and for all that we are *not alone*. When our homes are being threatened and our jobs are on the line, it is time to raise up our hands in prayer for deliverance. When our men are addicted to dope and they feel there is no hope, it is time to lift up hands that cry for mercy. And if they cannot raise them alone, we in the brotherhood must *be there* to lend our brother a hand.

Wanted: Model Fathers

Right now, God is calling our men to prayer and study. We talk about praying, but it is often all talk. Our men need to bathe their homes, their wives, and their children in prayer. A man ought to wake up in the morning with his family. The first words out of his mouth should not be *"Good Morning, America,"* but *"Good Morning, Lord."* Our Afrikan-American men must become model fathers, not model failures. They must recognize that attitudes are caught more quickly than they are taught. The responsibility of a father starts early and ends late. God, teach the heads of our families to pray with their families. May they be *one* with their wives. May they learn the eternal truth that asks the question...*How shall two walk together unless they be agreed?* Give our men the wisdom to know that if their hands are not raised, the enemy will prevail. Give them the insight to know that God will enter into the battle for them. May Black fathers discover that when they pray they become channels for the power and mercy of a loving God. May Black husbands be aware that when they pray, the devil cannot stand it because he knows they have more in them now than they ever had before. And may they learn the divine, historically validated lesson that *if God be for them, he's more than the world against them.*

When men start to pray and lift up their hands, an enormous event begins to take place in their lives—just as Moses became the conduit for God's power when his hands were raised to the heavens. Here is what will happen. When men raise their hands in prayer, God will intervene and they, like the children of Israel, will begin winning the battle. But it is not just the man who wins; the entire family will start winning, jobs will start winning, the bank account will start winning. When men start praying in their homes, something else is going to happen. The devil is going to start running, and demons will start scurrying. But this will happen only when God's men rise up and start praying.

We need fathers whom the spoils of office cannot buy. We need men who refuse to cheat and who will not lie. We need men who are strong—strong enough to know they can't do it all alone. Our brothers must pray. Our sisters must pray. We *all* must pray just to make it today. And when the results of those prayers begin to take effect, it becomes a sight to behold as the enemy host squirms, and their chariots turn, and their stomachs churn. Why? Because men are praying for the Lord of hosts to give them the courage to fight on. Suddenly, the "battle begins to shift hands." The forces of the enemy start to lose their footing, and the man of God who is a representative of the people of God suddenly feels the strength of a Samson. When men pray, their places of business will gain strength, their children will gain strength, and the relationship with their wives will gain strength. When Black men pray, their little Black boys will rise up and call them blessed. When men pray, their grandchildren will understand that granddaddy is God's man.

Men, in God's name be strong. Fight the battle. Get into the fray and make this the day that turns your life around. Moses held up his hands and Israel prevailed. When he let down his hands, the enemy prevailed. That is not some nostalgic message from an obscure passage in an ancient manuscript. This is counsel from God's word, and fresher, more encouraging—and much more redeeming—than today's headlines! It was written for all of us to believe and live today.

Power from on High

Power for our men is going to come in many ways. At times it will come through courage, at times through confidence, sometimes through perseverance, and sometimes just by having *staying power*. Oftentimes power will come through a dramatic change of attitude—when we quit the *blame game* and start playing the *I am responsible game*. But however the power falls, our men must pray for God's best, and settle for nothing less. It has been true throughout the ages: when we work, we work; when we pray, God works. He may say yes, he may say no, or he may say wait a while. But he will respond to any request asked in faith and uttered in his name. Moses knew the power of God. Joshua knew the power of prayer. The question we must ask ourselves is: do we know the power of prayer and the potential it will bring to our lives?

Dare, Dare, Dare

In closing, let us give a mandate to the hope of our race, the Afrikan-American husband and father whom we command to dare to move beyond the limited ideas of others. To dare to think for himself. To dare to think for the future. To dare to conceive of a world where he will be more than a consumer, and more than a clown draped in purple. To dare to stop wearing odd clothes and start finding his glory in being Black. To dare to stretch his imagination. To dare to see beauty as a norm. To dare to be beautiful. To dare to be creatively free. To dare to be a creative fire. To dare to quiet life fighters with a smile.

Dare, my brother. Our race depends on your courage. Our nation awaits your answer. Our church must have your reply. Dare to rise up, O man of God. It is not only the Marines who are looking for a "few good men." God, too, is looking for that faithful few who will do his bidding in their lives. "Rise up," the hymn writer William Merrill says,

> Rise up, O men of God! Have done with lesser things;
> Give heart and soul and mind and strength to serve the
>   King of kings.
>
> Rise up, O men of God! His kingdom tarries long;
> Bring in the day of brotherhood, and end the night of
>   wrong.
>
> Rise up, O men of God! The church for you doth wait,
> Her strength unequal to her task; rise up and make her
>   great!
>
> Lift high the cross of Christ;
> Tread where his feet have trod;
>   As brothers of the Son of man,
> Rise up, [rise up,] O men of God!

Today is the day. Now is the hour. Lift up your hands in prayer to God. Lift your hands for the Savior to see. Lift him up as Lord and Master of your work, your home and every other area of your life. In the Garden of Gethsemane, Jesus had time to think about how folks lied about him, talked mean about him, misused him, and abused him. But Jesus understood that if he could just lift up his hands, then behind every dark cloud there would be a silver lining. If he could just lift up his hands, God would move on his behalf. If he could just lift up his hands, the angels in his Father's heaven would watch over him. So when his hands got heavy, goodness and mercy appeared and lifted the hands of our loving Lord.

There is the story of the five ships anchored in the bay of a large seaport. A raging storm was gathering offshore. One captain and his ship decided to run not away from the storm but into it. Everything was fastened down and everyone was on their knees in prayer. Out into the stormy sea they went—reeling and rocking, pitching and tossing. The old ship did everything but go down. A couple of days later, battered but not broken, she returned to port to find the other ships broken on the beach.

The storm of all ages is raging. Let us run not away from it, but into it. The church needs to take the offensive and trust the Captain who still has the power to say, "Peace, be still." Now is the time to launch out into the deep. This is the time to lift up your hands and experience the power that will overtake you for now and eternity. Be strong in his might. Be strong in his grace. The battle is yours. The enemy is defeated. *Rise up, for you are a man of God!*

Keeping a Promise

Titus H. James

Titus James is pastor of Northside Heights Christian Church in Wichita, Kansas. Titus graduated from Jarvis Christian College and Pacific School of Religion.

Genesis 21:1–3*

Sarah had a baby! She must have been in her eighties or nineties. Abraham, her husband, was one hundred years old. This should have been impossible. When you are this old, love and affection are possible. It may be a miracle, but it is possible. But conception after being barren so long, enduring nine months of pregnancy and actually giving natural childbirth would be next to impossible.

This real old couple had a baby boy. They named him Isaac. As far as we could tell by this brief report, both mother and baby were doing fine.

---

*The scripture references in this sermon are from the King James Version of the Bible.

Genesis 21:1 says: "And the Lord visited Sarah as he had said, and the LORD did unto Sarah as he had spoken." God will do what he said he would do.

A promise, great or small, is significant. For a promise builds hope and expectations for something good to happen in the future. It's a joy to read of this great promise of a son to Abraham and Sarah kept by God. It had taken twenty-five eventful years but God kept his promise. Sarah grew a little impatient during the twenty-five-year period and picked a slave girl to have a child for her and Abraham. This was not the plan or promise; even so, God kept his promise. Sarah had a baby! Naturally the future of Abraham and Sarah was brightened. It can truthfully be stated that the future of the whole world was blessed because God kept his promise.

The birth of Isaac, whose name means "laughter," brought joyous praise to God. The birth of Isaac began the great promise God made unto Abraham. It was promised Abraham would be the father of a multitude and of many nations. God promised him sons who would be kings. He was promised a royal heritage.

Great kings are in the lineage of Abraham. There was Saul, the first king of Israel; David, the great conquering king; and Solomon, a wise and noble king, who brought Israel to a state of wealth and prosperity like none the world had ever seen. In the bloodline of Abraham, in the lineage of Isaac, is the person Jesus the Christ. Today he reigns as King of kings and Lord of lords. God is keeping his promise.

The whole world was blessed when God kept his promise to Abraham and Sarah. All future generations can be inspired by the faith of Abraham. We can learn that it's best to wait on God by the acts of King Saul. We can be encouraged and even humbled by the life and trials of King David. We gain wisdom, instruction, and fortitude from the words of King Solomon. We are saved unto eternal life through Jesus Christ our Lord. All of these wonderful works of life, influenced by kings, are ours to have because God kept his promise. Aren't you glad that God will do what he said he would do?

When promises are broken or they go unfulfilled, it is so disappointing. You ever have somebody borrow your money and promise to pay you back on payday and they fail to do what they promised? Does that make you happy? No, it doesn't. It makes you mad. You get upset with that person and you may even lose trust in him.

As we approach the end of the twentieth century we see the institution of the family dismantled and growing void of parental influence. The institution of the family is dissolving from within. This is happening because so many promises are not being kept at home. When a couple is married and they promise to love and cherish one another but break that promise there will probably be a breakdown in the family. In this day and time more than 50 percent of all marriages end in divorce. Divorce is a broken promise to God and to all the witnesses who attended the wedding.

Our families also suffer and fall apart because of broken promises involving problems that plague our community. You hear it and see it every day: "I'll quit tomorrow" or "I won't drink and drive" or "I'm gonna get help for my drug problem real soon" and "I'm gonna get a job." Society wants people to promise not to have sex until they are responsible. God would have us promise not to have sex until marriage. These broken promises wreak havoc within our families. We see lives ruined. People become homeless; they are forced to live in poverty. We see teenagers demanding abortions. We are shocked at all the sad and violent deaths that are so unnecessary. All this hurt and grief because of broken promises.

Is it so hard to keep a promise? After all, it took God Almighty twenty-five years to keep his promise with Abraham and Sarah. I suggest that it is not hard to keep a promise. What is hard is submitting to the command and commitments of the promise. When we forget, fail, or choose not to follow through on a promise it's broken. Is it because it's just too difficult?

Today we are living under the influence of broken treaties with the American Indians and the nonpayment of the forty acres and a mule promised to many of the African-American freed slaves. These were broken promises indeed, but we have a special promise from God in 2 Chronicles 7:14. God promised to hear from heaven, forgive our sin, and heal our land.

This indeed is a special promise. It is not impossible for God to keep or to fulfill. From heaven God hears and answers our prayers. It's a comfort knowing that our prayers for the world, for the children, and for ourselves are being answered by God. The forgiveness of our sins is a blessing we desperately need. For the wages of sin is death, but the gift of God, the promise of God, is eternal life. God has promised all of this to us. Can you say, "Thanks be to God"? For God will do what he said he would do. The healing of our land may be difficult to imagine, but I believe God can heal our land. The closing of the savings and loans, the gang violence, the AIDS epidemic, and the prison overcrowding can be healed.

These precious promises of 2 Chronicles 7:14 begin with the word *If*. This word presents a condition involving a mutual effort on the part of God and the people. If the people will humble themselves and pray, if they will seek God's face and turn from their wicked ways then God will keep his promises.

The question that is before us now is, will the people or will the church keep its part of the promise? Have you as a Christian believer ever made a promise to God? Perhaps we should make a promise to God. Our custom is to receive new members by the confession of faith. We don't ask if they promise to be righteous and holy members of the church. We don't even ask if they promise to pay all their tithe to the Lord. We don't even ask if they will be in church every Sunday and be here on time. We are just glad to have them join and then we rejoice with the angels in heaven. Maybe this church needs to make a promise to God. Can we promise to fulfill the expectations of God found in 2 Chronicles 7:14? They are clear and easy to follow.

All who are willing to make this promise to God please stand and repeat after me: "O Lord God, the Father of Abraham, Isaac, Jacob, and Jesus, I (state your name) promise this day to humble myself and pray. I promise to seek your face and turn from my wicked ways so that you will hear from heaven, forgive my sins, and heal my land. Amen."

Do you know what we just did? We just made a promise to God. We just promised God that we will humble ourselves and pray. Humbling ourselves we are to live lowly and meek. That's all right, because when we live like that we don't think we are better than anybody else. We know we have no merit in the eyes of God. We are free of vanity. This is essential for discipleship. We have got to humble ourselves.

Praying should be an easy promise. We ought to always pray. We are to be glad to spend time with God in prayer. Just take the time to listen to and talk with God. Ask God's mercy for others; listen to what the Spirit is saying to the church and to you. The word of God is truth and it does come back to remembrance. We have got to pray. Try spending as much time in prayer as you do on the telephone. It will change your life.

We are to seek God's face. Try to enter his presence by acknowledging God in all that we do. Look to see his goodness around you and in the lives of others and when you notice his handiwork or miracles or blessings, give him the praise. Seek to have his face show up on your face. Live out the will of God through holiness and righteousness.

To keep this all-important promise to God we have got to go all the way. We must turn from our wicked ways. It gets easy now, doesn't it? No, no, here is where the task gets tough. Can you turn from your wicked ways as you have just promised? I'm glad you can. To turn from our wicked ways means to stop sinful ways of our life. We have to change as people of pride and pleasure to a people of holiness. We have to repent of our sin. Praise God. True repentance is the actual turning from our wicked ways. Can you keep this promise? God will do what he said he will do! What about you?

Church, can you keep this promise? I believe we can. Paul would have us to know that we as a church can do all things through Christ who loves us. We as a church together, on one face, and all of us, leaving no one out, all of us together can turn from our wicked ways. We as a church can keep this promise. If we did it would be beautiful. It would help clean up the church house and a major portion of the community. If we just keep this promise.

If we keep this promise God will keep his promise. God will do what he said he will do. This promise may have been recorded a long time ago but it is still valid. God will hear from heaven, God will forgive our sins and heal our land. This promissory note can be cashed at the bank of glory by the riches of Jesus Christ, the Son of the living God. God will keep his promise!

God's promises are true. Second Corinthians 1:20: "For all the promises of God in him are yea, and in him amen, unto the glory of God by us." In Jesus the promises of God are available to you. They are given in the affirmative. They are yes and amen. If you need a promise the answer is yes and so be it. If God promised it, yes, you can have it.

Joshua 23:10: "One man of you shall chase a thousand: for the LORD your God, he it is that fighteth for you, as he hath promised you." The Lord will fight your battles just like he promised. When God is fighting he will always win. He'll fight your battle if you will fight. The problem is we don't want to fight. Do you have a battle on your hands? Is the fight worth fighting? If it is, let the Lord fight your battle. Let him do it. He'll win and you will win.

First John 1:9: "If we confess our sins, he is faithful and just to forgive us our sins, and to cleanse us from all unrighteousness." This is a very precious promise. I would perish were it not for this promise. I'm glad I know about forgiveness. This is the knowledge that keeps me from death, hell, and destruction. Jesus shed his blood to keep this promise. By his blood we are made clean. We're washed in that crimson flow and lose all our guilty stains.

Jesus promised that one day, as noted by John 14:3: "I will come again, and receive you unto myself." This is a loving promise that every child of God wants kept in his life. Jesus will receive us unto himself. He will keep us forever. Thank God for this promise. He may receive me when I die. He may receive me in the rapture, or the Lord may meet me in the air. However he receives me, it's all right because the Lord will do what he said he will do!

Church, dear congregation, would you please stand with me and read with me Romans 4:13–16? Having read this, don't you see that the promises of God are for all? If you have faith in God, keep trusting his promises. The goodness of God is promised unto all of us.

Only the Almighty God can keep such promises as he did with Abraham. This same loving God can keep his promises with all of you. Amen.

$\mathcal{T}$hrough It All, Trust in God

Rufus Lewis

Rufus Lewis is pastor of Macedonia Christian
Church in Birmingham, Alabama. He is a graduate of
Miles College in Birmingham and is currently attending
Beeson Divinity School. In addition, Rufus is
currently serving as the first
Black moderator of his region,
the Christian Church (Disciples of Christ)
in Alabama-Northwest Florida.

Hebrews 12:1–13

In Hebrews 12, the author speaks in his letter to Hebrew Christians. He talks about their complaints: bad days and hard times. They have almost given up on running the Christian race.

Obviously, they had not heard that song, "I won't complain." For in that song the writer says, "When I look around and think things over, I find that my good days outweigh my bad days so I won't complain." I think he has a good point.

In this letter, the writer reminds these Christians of those dedicated and committed Christians who had gone before them—how they had paid the price, endured the pain, suffered, and died; and yet they looked over into the promised land, but they did not go. But because of their faith *in God*, they endured the hardships of life for God, and they stayed in the race with God.

And, then he reminded them that what they were presently going through, and that which the Christian witnesses before them had gone through, did not compare with the pain, agony, and suffering that Jesus endured for our sins. They, you, and we might have some bad days, but we have not shed blood, we have no nail prints, we have not been pierced and we have not died.

Then they are reminded of God's word in Proverbs 3:11–12:

My child, do not despise the LORD's discipline
    or be weary of his reproof,
for the LORD reproves the one he loves,
    as a father the son in whom he delights.

In other words, the Lord allows some things to happen to us because he loves us, and because he is getting us ready for something better that is on the way. We are told in Hebrews 12:11:

Now, discipline always seems painful rather than pleasant at the time, but later it yields the peaceful fruit of righteousness to those who have been trained by it.

Like the Hebrew Christians, the Macedonian Christians are the same way. Sometimes we want to give up on life. We get upset and downset; depressed and oppressed; despondent and dejected; headache, heartache, and toothache; gingivitis, hepatitis, and arthritis; footsores, buttsores, and bedsores; don't wanna go, can't go, and refuse to go. And it's never because of anything we have done, but it is always because of everything everybody else has done, and so we are ready to give up on life.

But the writer of Hebrews is trying to tell us something. When we have trials and tribulations in life, it's a reminder that we are children of God, loved by God, cared for by God, and therefore disciplined by God.

We ought to be thankful for our problems: if we never have a problem, we would not know that there is a Problem Solver.

If you've never been down, you don't know how it feels to be up.

If you've never been sick, you can't understand why we call God "Doctor Jesus."

If you've never been rained on , you can't appreciate the sun.

It is still true: no cross, no crown.

When you have not lied, been lied on, or lied to, your appreciation for the truth is limited. People in jail can appreciate freedom with a passion, and when you've been in the valley of hell, you long for the mountain of heaven.

One of the mistakes parents make is the failure to discipline their children. There is no greater love than the love of God, and the Bible says that God disciplines those he loves, i.e., when we fail to let our children have some bad days, this is a showing of no love. I have heard parents say, "I don't want my child to come up like I did." What's wrong with the way you came up? There were times when you didn't have what you wanted, but you had what you needed. Sometimes you had to walk where you had to go, but you got there. You remember the days when you couldn't see your way through, but you made it. God permitted us to witness the dark so we could appreciate the light. Your child can't appreciate *anything* because you have tried to give him *everything*. If you fail to let your child crawl, she will have a hard time trying to walk. Last week a young man told me that he lost his job because he had no transportation and before I knew it, I heard myself say, "Hell, what's wrong with your feet?"

Many of our children are on Tylenol, aspirin, pot, cocaine, and other drugs to keep from facing the hardships and hard times in life. They fail to learn that night comes before day; that you must crawl before you walk; that rocky roads will lead you to paved roads; that good times come as a result of bad times; and that when we trust in Jesus Christ, and wait on the Lord, God will make everything just right.

We are told in verses 12 and 13, "Therefore lift your drooping hands and strengthen your weak knees, and make straight paths for your feet, so that what is lame may not be put out of joint, but rather be healed."

Let us not cause our children to have drooping hands and feeble arms and weak knees. Don't you be responsible for your child being lame and disabled. Let the hard times and the hardships come, and when it is over, your child and my child will be able to say, "Through it all, I've learned to trust in Jesus." Amen.

A Soul Is a Terrible Thing to Waste

Rosetta Robinson

Rosetta Robinson is a senior seminarian at Howard University Divinity School. A member of Twelfth Street Christian Church in Washington, D.C., Rosetta serves as associate minister of Plymouth Congregational Church in Washington.

Matthew 25

Every time I see a particular commercial on television about us African Americans, and our particular need for equal education, because of our particular experience in a particular country called America, it gets my attention. It gets my attention because I don't have to go too far to find a similar example in my own community of someone who wants to go to college but can't afford to.

Perhaps if you're like me you sympathize with young black men and women who are trying to better themselves by trying to get into college. You identify with the meaning of the slogan, "A Mind Is a Terrible Thing to Waste." And so it is.

While a mind is a terrible thing to waste, I'm one of those peculiar people always concerned about something else, that has eternal ramifications. You see, from my understanding, "A Soul Is a Terrible Thing to Waste."

Can you say, "Amen!" If you give me a few moments, I'd like to reflect on that through the twenty-fifth chapter of Matthew.

Wasting things is nothing new to human beings. I can recall my mother saying don't waste your food and don't waste time. Conservationists tell us don't waste gas, don't waste the water, and don't waste energy. Even Jesus, in our text, gives us some figurative examples of folks who wasted things.

Matthew 25 begins with the parable of the ten maidens at the wedding feast. In Jesus' day, as in ours, everybody loves a wedding. Using the example of a wedding was a good way to get a point across. In the Jewish custom of that time, the groom brought his bride from her parents' home to his own. Jesus describes the wedding scene prior to the arrival of the groom. We'll come back to this story. I want to move to the next parable.

The second parable is also about a subject people love, and love too much: money. They'll steal, kill, lie, and die for it. Jesus again turns to a familiar subject to teach a mysterious lesson. He introduces us to three servants, and what they do with the money they get from their master.

The text tells us of a man who went on a journey and left his servants with some of his property. Matthew 25:15 says, "To one he gave five talents, to another two, to another one, to each according to his ability. Then he went away."

Two of the servants did some trading with the money, and made a profit, doubling their original sum. The one who received two talents made two more, and the one who started out with five earned five more. But that third servant, he was probably a little more like us. He was a bit stingy—so he hides his money.

Now a talent was worth about fifteen years' wages. Some scholars think it was about a thousand dollars. So in those days it was a lot of money. The one who received the smallest sum hides it, you know, like Black people have been known to do, hiding money under mattresses and in shoeboxes. The stingy man's stingy attitude backfires on him. Not only is the money tucked away in a place where it can't draw interest or be invested, this servant ends up losing what he was trying to save.

Listen to what the Master says to him: "You ought to have invested my money with the bankers, and on my return I would have received what was my own with interest. So take the talent from him, and give it to the one with the ten talents." You can hold on to your money if you want to, but when you die somebody else will get what you don't spend.

This twenty-fifth chapter of Matthew doesn't stop here. We go from ten foolish maidens, to a stingy servant, to smelly goats. This third parable, the one that talks about the sheep and the goats, is the high point of Jesus' discourse, of his religious instruction to his disciples. This parable is called the parable or judgment of the nations. It's essentially about priorities, about people living out their faith, about spiritual rewards. Jesus uses double-talk to point out that human beings can have their earthly existence and all that comes from it, yet lack merit in the final judgment.

The ones who get the best reward for their efforts are called the sheep who know God's voice. The ones who don't, well, they're just, in Jesus' talk, unrighteous goats. They are the stench in God's nostrils. They're all talk and no action. You know those kinds of folks.

Smelly goats, a stingy servant, and ten foolish maidens. What do they have in common?

In all three parables, there are winners and losers. Since most of us want to be winners, we can learn something from these stories. The winners in the first parable are the five wise women who kept their lamps filled with oil. They kept the faith, so that at whatever hour the bridegroom arrived, they'd be ready to meet him at the door, ready to go in to the feast. The losers didn't do that. They got lazy waiting. They slept too long. They let their oil run out. They were too busy doing other things to make preparations to see their way through the dark.

Too busy to catch hold of the everlasting light. And at midnight, when the bridegroom came, they had to run out to buy the oil they should have gotten a long time ago to see where they were going. But they were too late. They missed him. The door to the bridegroom's house was shut. They missed their chance to go the bridegroom's house, which symbolized the heavenly kingdom. The foolish maidens cried: "Lord, Lord, open to us," but the bridegroom, replied, "Truly, I say to you, I do not know you."

It's a terrible thing to hear the Lord say, "I do not know you. You've been a church member all your life. But I don't know you. You just don't act like one of my sheep."

Yes, a soul is a terrible thing to waste. Don't waste precious time arguing with God about who deserves a place in God's heaven. That's God's sovereign decision. Just be faithful. You can keep your oil burning brightly until he comes. You can be a witness until the bridegroom comes.

Yes, a soul is a terrible thing to waste.

The foolish maidens lost out. The man with the one talent in the second parable, he lost out too. The parable of the ten talents warns us not to be stingy with God's resources. The servant thought the Master was too hard, to ask him to get a new attitude about money. He was too attached to money. He fell into the trap of wanting to store up treasures on earth and not in heaven. So he was looking for any excuse to hold back.

We're that way whenever it comes to giving to the church. Won't we find any excuse to hold on to our church dollar! You can't beat God's giving no matter how hard you try.

Don't mess around trying to gain the whole world and neglect the important things. The things of the spirit. The internal and eternal. The things the Lord Jesus expects of his sheep.

What does the Lord require? The last parable is the one that reminds me and you, lest we forget, when it comes to picking sheep, God is searching for something on the inside. Jesus is interested in the way you show your love to God and to others. He wants to know: what did you do when I was hungry, when I was thirsty, when I was sick, when I was in prison?

Our prisons are full of African-American males. National statistics show one in four black males is in prison, or in jail, or on parole. Most of us know a whole lot of somebodies in prison, in fact some of them are our own relatives; caught up in the web of what many call an unjust justice system for black males. Yet, too few of our churches have prison ministries.

You may wonder, "Jesus, what are you talking about? Lord, when did we see thee hungry and feed thee, or thirsty and give thee drink? And when did we see thee a stranger and welcome thee, or naked and clothe thee, and when did we see thee sick or in prison and visit thee?" Jesus has the answer: "Whatever you did not do for the least of these, you did not do it for me."

A soul is a terrible thing to waste.

We black folk have been accused of wasting time, money, and opportunities to help ourselves. We've been making a whole lot of other folks rich, while our communities are cut off from the resources they need to thrive, rather than waste away.

Listen, I'm here today because I love you, because I care about your soul.

Let me put you in touch with someone who knows how to maximize human potential, someone who knows just what to do with souls. If you invest in this person, you invest in eternity.

I know how easy it is to get sidetracked. To get hung up with the wrong crowd doing all the wrong things at midnight, to waste time searching for the truth in all the wrong places. Search no more.

There's nobody like Jesus. Jesus is the way, the truth, and the life. There's none like him. He's our righteousness, he is the Rock of Ages, the Cornerstone, Alpha and Omega, Bright and Morning Star, Lily of the Valley. He is the Word, the Lamb of God, he is the Oil of Salvation, he'll fill your cup and make it overflow, over and over and over again.

I'll take every blessing Jesus is offering and run with it. I'll take his peace. I'll take his joy. I'll take his grace. I'll take his love. You know he's mighty sweet. I'll take his mercy. I'll put on his name. I'll give cheerfully. I'll treat my neighbor right. I'll walk in his footsteps. And I'll take one of those mansions he says has been prepared for me in glory.

In this twenty-fifth chapter of Matthew, Jesus speaks in symbolic language about the last days—eschatology—the time when he will return to earth in all of his glory. He says there will be some signs, but they won't give you an exact day or hour. His message in the parable of the ten maidens and to all of us is to keep watching and waiting. The bridegroom will come when you least expect it. Just be ready.

Yes, a soul is a terrible thing to waste. Just be ready. Then you can look forward one day to hearing God say: "Well done, good and faithful servant, you have been faithful over a few things, I will make you ruler over many things, enter into the joy of the Lord. I saw you when you took my love to the sick, and the poor, and the discouraged. I saw you feeding the homeless, ministering to those in prison. I see your heart, I know you love me. I watched you go when no one else would. I've watched you step out on faith. Come, O blessed of my Father, inherit the kingdom prepared for you from the foundation of the world. Come and be blessed."

On Being a Magnet Church

Samuel W. Hylton, Jr.

Samuel Hylton is the longtime pastor of Centennial
Christian Church in St. Louis, Missouri. A graduate of
Winston-Salem University, Sam also studied religion at
Butler University.

John 12:32

And I, when I am lifted up from the earth, will draw all
people to myself.

A magnet is a body which has the property of attracting
iron and producing a magnetic field external to itself. A magnet draws and attracts.

The magnet school has become an important part of public
education in the United States of America. School administra-
tors take a school, remodel the building, enrich the curricula
offerings and place a strong faculty in it. The school becomes so
inviting and appealing that it attracts and pulls in students
from near and far. That is the magnet school concept.

I'm prepared to say that if the world is to be saved, if the
Christian faith is to make a durable impact upon society, our
task is to develop a magnet church that is so powerful that it

attracts and draws people into its life. Part of the reason for the ineffectiveness of the church is that while the world does not find any fault in Jesus Christ, it does find fault in the church as an institution or organization. John 12:32 casts a light on the problem of credibility on the part of the institutional church and personal faith. Jesus was addressing a party from Greece as well as Philip and Andrew who had introduced the Greeks to him. Jesus declares that he will not seek to avoid death on the cross because, as he said, "For this purpose I have come to this hour." Then he declares, "And I, when I am lifted up from the earth, will draw all people to myself."

This scripture calls our attention to the magnetism of Christ, the drawing or pulling power of Christ to attract people to himself. Just as a lodestone has the property to attract similar objects, Christ has the spiritual power to draw humankind. "If I am lifted up," says Jesus, "I will draw all people to myself."

The bad news is that the world in which we live is one of darkness and despair. The good news is that Jesus Christ is the light and hope of the world. The crucial need of our day is the need to rediscover that Christ is still mighty enough to save and still strong enough to carry the crushing burden of this world on his shoulder. If Christ is to do this, if Christ is to conquer this world, then it is our task both as individual Christians and as the corporate church to lift him up in the fullness of his stature.

But observe that Christ did not say that *we are to lift ourselves up,* but we are *to lift him up.* Our mission is not to draw attention to ourselves or to the church but to draw attention to him on the cross. There is no spiritual attraction, no divine magnet like Christ. The power that pulls and draws people to salvation is not what we do in our frail efforts but in what Christ has already done. We did not come to this worship service to praise ourselves but to praise God. My motivation in preaching this sermon is not to plead with Christ to save us but to thank him for already saving us.

How to reach the masses, men of every birth,
For an answer, Jesus gave the Key;
"And if I be lifted up from the earth,
Will draw all men unto me."

Don't exalt the preacher, don't exalt the pew,
Preach the gospel simple, full and free;
Prove him and you will find that the promise is true.
"I'll draw all men unto me."

Now if the church is to be a magnet church and lift Christ up, there are several things that must be considered. In the first place, if we do develop a magnet church we must again place more emphasis on the Bible and regard for the Holy Scriptures as the foundation of the community of faith. If we are to recapture the spirit and power of God to change the thought, if we are to let the spirit and power of God capture us, we must begin to read and study and live the Bible. As Paul wrote in 2 Timothy 2:15, "Do your best to present yourself to God as one approved by him, a worker who has no need to be ashamed, rightly explaining the word of truth."

By reading, studying, and living the Bible, we do not mean in a superficial way or manner. The Bible must be read, studied, and lived in a serious, responsible way. Too many church members know what the Bible says in a literal way, but do not know what it means. Our churches are populated with people who claim to know and believe in the Bible yet live lives of greed, bigotry, and self-righteousness. The old spiritual reminds us that "everybody talkin' about heaven ain't going there."

I am reminded of the story of the minister who went to visit a family. When he was ready to go, he said, "I want to read from the Scriptures and pray, but I left my Bible in my car and I would like to use one of your Bibles." The mother said, "Yes, Reverend," and said to one of the children, "Honey, go upstairs to the bedroom and bring that book that we love so well." The little girl went upstairs and when she came back she had a copy of the Sears and Roebuck catalog in her hand.

This story points out the present attitude and practice as it relates to the Bible. We give lip service to the Bible but do not give it the rightful place in our lives. Beware of talking about how much you honor and love the Bible and then proceed to ignore and neglect it. One of the reasons why we as individual Christians and as the collective church do not lift up Christ is because we have not placed the proper emphasis on the Holy Scriptures. The church cannot possess the power of God as long as it neglects the Book which can supply the power. A study indicates that most churches have fewer than 10 percent of their members in active Bible study. If the church is to be magnetic it must again consider the Bible to be the foundation of the community of faith.

In the second place, if the church is to be magnetic and lift up Christ, it must show love and demonstrate compassion. Compassion is the value that sets the church apart as God's people. Karen Armstrong has written in her book *The History of God* that "the authentic test of a religion is not what we believe but what we do." Unless our religion expresses itself in compassion, it is not real. Of course, this insight is not new. This is precisely what the apostle Paul was writing in 1 Corinthians 13:1–13, the point being that as Christians we can be eloquent, have great faith, and even give our bodies to be burned, but if we have not loved we are nothing at all. Tough words, you say, but it is the truth.

We must be willing to demonstrate compassion for all kinds of people. People may say all sorts of things about us, do all kinds of things against us, but if we are Christians we have to love them just the same. Jesus never said that everyone would be lovable. And a lot of people are unlovable but we have to love them just the same.

And this love includes people who share life within the fellowship of the church. People in the church make mistakes, commit sins, just like people who do not belong to the church. And when people sin who do belong to the church, forgiveness, not condemnation, is in order. Keith Miller reminds us that the church is the only army that shoots its wounded. When our sisters and brothers in the church fall down, our task is to help them up, not kick them. This is the Christian way. This is God's way. We help people with love, not hate. We redeem people not with pressure but with prayer. We lift Christ up not by gossiping about people but by expressing grace. We lift Christ up by demonstrating the principles of compassion and love.

Finally, we develop a magnet church and lift Christ up by showing interest in and concern for the world. Christ wants us to love the church, but he wants us to love the world enough that we will want all people to know Christ and to be drawn unto him. John 3:16 states, "For God so loved the world that he gave his only Son, so that everyone who believes in him may not perish but may have eternal life." So we lift Christ up by opening the windows and doors of the church and carrying the message of the gospel out of the church into the world.

It is told that Robert Louis Stevenson at the age of twelve was looking out into the darkness from his upstairs room, watching a man lighting the street lamps. Stevenson's mother called and asked him what he was doing. He answered, "Mother, I am watching a man cut holes in the darkness." That is our mission, to cut holes in the darkness. We must build the magnet church as we lift Christ up by cutting holes in the darkness.

$\mathcal{R}$obbery Without a Weapon

Alvin O. Jackson

Alvin O'Neal Jackson is the pastor of the largest congregation of the Christian Church (Disciples of Christ), Mississippi Boulevard Christian Church in Memphis, Tennessee. Alvin has degrees from Duke University Divinity School and United Theological Seminary of Dayton, Ohio.

Malachi 3:7–12*

Have you heard that on January 16, 1994, at 70 North Bellevue, the Mississippi Boulevard Christian Church, Memphis, Tennessee, around 11:30 a.m. a robbery was committed? An undetermined amount of money was stolen. This doesn't appear to be the first time that this crime was committed. The evidence strongly suggests that this is only one of many unchecked offenses that have been going on over a long period of time. The evidence also suggests that it was an inside job. There were no signs of forced entry. Thirty-five hundred people were present at the scene of the crime and at least three thousand are suspected of actively participating in the rob-

---

*The scripture references in this sermon are from the King James Version of the Bible.

bery. None of the suspects has been apprehended. The authorities are still investigating.

One of the authorities commented that in all of his years of investigating robberies, he has never seen anything like this one before. A large sum of money is missing, but no money seems to have changed hands. The money appears to have been stolen from God...address unknown. No indication of weapons used and no visible signs of a struggle. It appears to have been a robbery without a weapon.

I have just come today on behalf of the authorities to issue the warrants for arrest. But I have also come to announce that the Judge in the case, who is also God, is willing to suspend the sentences and pardon all who will make a vow never to commit this crime again.

This is the message that the prophet Malachi delivers to the people of Israel. We find in the book of Malachi that the prophet goes to the people in God's behalf. He is pleading with the people to return to God what they have taken from him. He reads God's love letter to them, expressing the pain of God's unrequited love. He says the Lord says: "I have loved you; I have delivered you; I am your parent; I am your partner; I entered into covenant with you; I married you. You became my people and I became your God, your companion, your keeper and provider; and yet you have despised me and dishonored me and withheld yourselves, your service and your substance from me who withholds nothing from you."

The relationship has been one-sided and one-sided relationships just don't work. We need to do all we can from our side, and on our part to keep open the channels between us and God. Healthy relationships cannot be one-sided. In the relationship between parents and children, both sides must be considerate of each other. In the relationship between a husband and wife, there are certain initiatives a wife must take and certain responses that a husband must make and vice-versa. If it is one-sided it will topple over. And if one-sided relationships do not work in human experience, what makes you think that one-sided relationships will work with respect to the structure and the function of the interaction that takes place between us and God? There is something that we must do in order to maintain a right relationship with God.

Malachi said in the first chapter of his book that a son honors his father and a servant respects his master, but the people of God despise God. The people said, "Well, how is it that we have despised you?" And the Lord answered, "You have offered polluted bread on my altar." You have given me trash and mess and refuse and dung and garbage. You have given me far less than your best. And that doesn't work with Uncle Sam. Try that for taxes or tuition or rent, or mortgage, or clothes, or the car note. All of these must consist of serious, regular, and substantial payment and yet we think we can stroll into the presence of the Almighty and do less for God than we do for ourselves, our conveniences, and our creature comforts.

The prophet Malachi declares that we have left God; we have departed from him; we are mouthing the words *I believe* but our actions are not consistent with what we are saying. But then the prophet comes to chapter 3, where he announces that God says to us, "If you will return to me, I will return to you." "If you do something, then I will do something." And it is at this point that the prophet says, "Will a man rob God?" Will anybody be so bold and brazen to rob the living God? Will people in their mortality and weakness and shortness and frailty and brevity of days on earth rob God, while they are open to all kinds of accidents and tragedies and contingencies and calamities and setbacks and illnesses and uncertainties? Will we in our weakness and vulnerability and dependency rob God? The God who owns and sustains the whole universe? Will we dare rob God?

The question is not whether a person will steal from God. For when you steal from somebody, that means you are taking from behind that person's back. The person from whom you steal can't see what you are doing. But when you rob somebody, you are doing it to their person, in their face. You are openly assaulting and assailing the victim. You are robbing and traumatizing a person in the person's presence. And so the question is will a person dare rob, assault, and assail the person of God? God, all-powerful, all-knowing, all-wise, all-loving, and everywhere present! Will anybody dare be that ungrateful?

Everything we have comes from God. We brought nothing into this world and we will take nothing out of it. There are no pockets in a shroud; no cash in a casket; and no Brink's truck in a funeral procession. If you have anything, God gave it to you! I know there are those who say, "I got it on my own; I did it for myself. I worked my job; I got up every morning and went to my job." But who woke you up? Who started you on your way? Who gave you strength to stand and life to live and breath to breathe and love to enjoy and hope to hold on to? Who opened the job door up for you and gave you the opportunity to work? The writer of the book of James says, "Every good gift and every perfect gift is from above, and cometh down from the Father of lights, with whom is no variableness, neither shadow of turning." Jesus said, "Freely you have received, freely give." And Paul said, "What have you got that you didn't receive?" When will we learn to shout like Paul, "I am what I am but by the grace of God!"

So God said to the people through Malachi, the prophet, you have robbed me. And the people said, "How have we robbed you?" And God said, you have done it by withholding your tithes and your offerings. And if you really want to mend your broken relationship with me, if you really want to keep faith with me, if you really want to pick up the pieces of your shattered life and put them back together again...here's how you do it, "Bring ye all the tithes into the storehouse," not just a little pinch of it all, but all. Don't hold back part of it. Pay the whole thing, the whole tenth, without robbing God, without cheating, without defrauding God. Malachi says, "Bring ye all the tithes into the storehouse." Now the word *storehouse* is translated from the Hebrew word that means the temple treasure. The same word is used in Nehemiah 13:12, which says they brought all Judah the tithe of the coin and the new wine and the oil into the treasury...which treasury? The United Way? Neighborhood Charities? March of Dimes? United Negro College Fund? NAACP? Black United Front? None of these!

The word means the treasuries of the house of God. The tithe is explicitly and exclusively a holy offering unto God through the institution of the congregation of the people of God...the church. This concept of the tithe is demonstrated and substantiated in Leviticus 27:30, which says the tithe is the Lord's. It is holy unto the Lord. And there is further documentation that the Hebrew word in Malachi that we translate as storehouse refers to the temple treasury, for 2 Chronicles 31:11 says, "Then Hezekiah commanded to prepare chambers in the house of the LORD; and they prepared them, and brought in the offerings and the tithes and the dedicated things faithfully." Thus, the tithe was not to be broken down by the person, or distributed in the community according to the notions and taste and priorities and pet projects and concerns of an individual. The tithe was to be brought into the house of the Lord and to be dedicated holy unto the Lord. Now, that much is explicit! That's not my opinion. It's in the Word. It's God's plan for the people of God.

Where shall we tithe? Not to the radio or television evangelist, because you are not going to call them when you get sick or when you need somebody to preach a relative's funeral, or when you need somebody to come to the hospital to see you. You are not going to call Billy Graham or Oral Roberts or Robert Schuller or any of those folks. You are going to call some preacher in town; you need to pay your tithe to a church in town. The church will always have sufficient resources to meet human needs and the name of the Lord will be exalted and the gospel will be preached and missions will grow throughout the world.

The tithe is a basic admission that God is the source of your life. And if you shout without bringing your tithe, you are shouting on credit! "Bring ye all the tithes into the storehouse." Yes, I believe that God had a place like Mississippi Boulevard Christian Church in mind when he said, "Bring ye all the tithes into the storehouse." Don't split it up, but let me make a powerful and meaningful impact upon the life of Memphis and the life of the world. Let it be a witness of life and hope. Let it be a light shining in the darkness of confusion and disruption. Let it be one place where young folks can come and be safe. Let it be one place where anybody can come and get a meal and help and hope and love and joy! Let it be a house of prayer for all nations! Let it be a rock in a weary land and a shelter in a time of storm!

"And prove me now herewith, saith the LORD of hosts." Prove me now! Let me demonstrate that I will "open you the windows of heaven, and pour out a blessing, that there shall not be room enough to receive it." The cry of the world is that we don't have enough. We don't have enough joy! We don't have enough peace! We don't have enough hope! But when we learn to trust God, when we stop robbing him, when we learn to seek him first, we will no longer have to cry not enough, but we will be able to shout not room enough! Lord, hasten that day! Amen.

$\mathcal{B}$read for the World

Clifford L. Willis

Clifford Willis is director of news and information for the Office of Communication of the Christian Church (Disciples of Christ). A graduate of Lincoln University, Cliff is a licensed minister currently serving in an additional capacity as interim minister of Fifth Christian Church, Cincinnati, Ohio.

John 6:1–5

Some of you will remember that "in another life" I was pastor of a country parish. You haven't lived if you've never experienced God in a rural church. Bill Cosby would say that "it's a different world than where you come from."

We didn't have many functional committees, we had no mission statement, and we didn't take pledges to meet the annual budget. But that congregation knew how to welcome strangers, love each other, and learned to be a church in mission. And that's not all. Those brothers and sister sure could set the table.

Having dinner at that little country church on Founders Day, Men's and Women's Day, or any other occasion was more than a meal—it was an experience. In fact, the food, fun, and fellowship flowed so freely it was almost sinful.

It seems to me that this kind of carrying on is part of our tradition. And if I'm right, there have been similar festive occasions here at Faith United.

More than once I've wanted to say grace over the day and go home instead of lead the next worship service. I don't know about you, but I just can't help myself, for that full feeling represents a kind of warmth, security, and satisfaction.

But the real sin is picked over, half-eaten food we throw away after church dinners and denominational gatherings. Countless families in Indianapolis, St. Louis, and elsewhere could live like nobility on our leavings. But they hunger for food and don't have the means to get it.

In 1990 13.5 percent of the 249 million U.S. residents lived below the poverty line: 31.9 percent were African American, 28.1 percent were Hispanic, 12.2 percent were elderly, and 44 percent of the children were Black.

Our work overseas helps us to know this kind of suffering isn't confined to North America. All across the world multitudes scuffle about, doing without so they and others they love might have bread.

In the '80s half or more of all residents in Lesotho lived in poverty; from 40 to 80 percent of folk in Zaire couldn't get safe water; and two thirds to three fourths of Salvadorans lived in absolute poverty.

So the question that remains is—"We have a crowd here who've been on the road a long time; how and where shall they buy bread to eat?" In other words, how do we provide "bread for the world"?

Our pericope finds Jesus doing ministry among the multitudes down by the seashore. He has heard their tales of woe and healed many of their afflictions when a matter just as pressing emerges—the need for food.

Jesus asks this bread question of Philip, his disciple, and he has no solution in mind. This is a teachable moment for Jesus. So while carrying out his own plan, the preacher uses this moment to teach the followers something about faith.

"Yes," says Philip, "how shall we buy bread? We've got more than five thousand men, women, and children here! It's getting late in the day, we're too far from town, and last but not least, we don't have enough money! Two hundred pennyworths or thirty dollars (U.S.) wouldn't buy everybody a little bit."

But disciples, then and now, forget that they keep company with Jesus—who also is God—Creator, Redeemer, and Sustainer of life. And where mere mortals may fail, with God, and even with Christ, all things are possible.

Jeremiah, the weeping prophet, declares: "O Lord GOD! It is you who made the heavens and the earth by your great power and by outstretched arm! Nothing is too hard for you."

Jesus also wants to teach the disciples that they must minister to the whole person. It's not enough to appeal only to the holiness of individuals. It's not enough to exorcise demons, forgive sins, and make the wounded whole, and to still allow suffering for the lack of bread. And this me-centered privatized religion that shows no concern for the neighbor has got to stop. Those who are concerned only with whether a soul is heaven-bound aren't much earthly good.

Jesus makes it abundantly clear that feeding the sheep is in each of our job descriptions. How can we speak of soul food when a family's shelves are bare and the children are malnourished?

James asks, what would you do if a brother or sister is poor, ill-clothed, and without food? Do you tell them to go in peace, be warm (or cool today), without meeting their needs? Faith without works is dead! We must feed them! If it is to be, it is up to me!

Christ asks, in another writer's account, what do we have then, seeing it's late, and we've no food nor money? What is available? "There is a boy here who has five barley loaves and two fish. But what are they among so many people?"

Can't you imagine the exchange between mother and son when he hears Jesus is in town? "Mom, Jesus is in revival this week. Can I go?" Mom consents and makes him a light meal to take along. She has no idea of her part in God's magnificent scheme.

Now the little boy hears the plight of the people with no provisions and offers all he has. He doesn't know that at any other time it wouldn't be enough. But in Jesus' hands a little becomes much, especially when one has the faith to give his all.

This is the second lesson. Use what you have! You see, though God can do anything, many times God won't until you first use what you have. If you want to solve the hunger problem, stop the drug epidemic or shelter the homeless, you can do it if you try. You gotta be able to say "something inside of me makes me feel like going ahead!"

You must do all you can do—then when you can't do any more or give any more—God will. God will make your burdens blessings, turn problems into possibilities, and transform tragedy into triumph. Humankind's extremity is God's opportunity.

Have you any rivers that you think are uncrossable? Have you any mountains that you cannot tunnel through? God specializes in things that seem impossible, and can do what no other power...no Holy Ghost power can do!

Second lesson—give the best you can. If God is important we can't give only leftovers of our time, talents, and finances. You don't invite someone to dinner, make them wait till dinner's done, and serve what's left. You want to give the best you can.

Then you give from the right perspective...not to earn a blessing, but to be a blessing. Sacrificial giving, such as the little boy did, never goes out of style.

When you give...God can open up the windows of heaven and pour you out a blessing your arms can't hold. Give and it'll be given back to you; "good measure, pressed down, shaken together," Luke says. There'll be an overrun of blessings in your life.

A little boy gave and Jesus received it and lifted it up. He blessed it by giving thanks and returned these elements—the fish and bread—back to the disciples. And as they shared, serving their neighbors first, then themselves, some way, somehow, there was enough for all.

Some scholars say that this sharing process, this business of feeding the neighbor first, is the key to the miracle. That's the third lesson. First others, then ourselves. That might be a good thing to do as we serve holy communion; serve others first, then ourselves; and watch God's grace abound in all our lives.

Scripture says they gathered the fragments, the leftovers, and had twelve basketfuls to share. You can do some creative things with left behinds. Congregations might replace mid-week family meals with "invite your neighbor out" dinners.

Use leftovers to jump start a hot-food bank or community feeding program. I don't know about the kitchen facilities, local ordinances, health restrictions involved. Just do it! The blessings will be enormous.

Try designated sharing. Ask that paid-for but uneaten dinners from regional/general meetings be given to a local homeless shelter or community-based feeding program.

Have a "mealless" meal once a day, or week, or whenever and donate the proceeds—the money you would have spent—to area feeding programs. The possibilities are endless.

And when we do that much and challenge our government not to make hungry, homeless, or hopeless people political pawns, then great masses of people can say along with Langston Hughes,"I, too, am America."

But let's not think that once the leftovers are gathered and distributed that the world's hunger problem is completely alleviated. There comes a time when Lean Cuisine or Hamburger Helper won't fill the void inside.

Wonder Bread won't do it when our spirits need sustenance. That bread never lasts anyway. People are hungering for good news about God and Jesus' love for all humanity. And if we don't also tell them about this love, we may provide valuable outreach programs, but fail at God's awesome project to preserve persons' souls and bodies.

Do you want to fill your soul's deepest longing? Turn it over to Jesus! He can feed a hungry people in a land of plenty. If we give our spiritual hunger to him we'll never want again. Christ is the one who can provide "Bread for the World."

> How to reach the masses, those of every birth
> for an answer Jesus gave the key.
> He said if I, if I be lifted up from the earth,
> I'll draw everyone unto me.

> Oh, the world is hungry for the Living Bread.
> Lift the Savior up for all to see.
> Trust him and do not doubt the words that he says,
> "I'll draw everyone unto me."

*W*hat's Love Got to Do with It?

Cynthia L. Hale

> *Cynthia Hale* is founding pastor of the Ray of Hope
> Christian Church in Decatur, Georgia. A former federal
> prison chaplain, she has degrees from Hollins College,
> Duke University, and United Theological Seminary.
> Cynthia has served as president of the
> ministers' fellowship of the
> National Convocation of the Christian Church,
> and is currently first vice moderator of the
> Christian Church (Disciples of Christ).

Romans 5:6–8

For while we were still weak, at the right time Christ
died for the ungodly. Indeed, rarely will anyone die for
a righteous person—though perhaps for a good person
someone might actually dare to die. But God proves his
love for us in that while we still were sinners Christ
died for us.

We live in a world that needs to know and understand real
love. People are hungry for love. The evidence is all around us,
among us, and even within us.

Several years ago, Dionne Warwick, among others, sang
the song, "What the world needs now is love, sweet love, not
just for some, but for everyone." Nothing has changed. We still
need love, now more than ever. With the increasing violence

in our streets and in our homes, particularly among our own, it's clear that we need more love.

If there were more love, there would be less disrespect and dehumanization of persons; there would be more giving and less taking. There wouldn't be so much loneliness and persons flocking to people, places, and things that promise to provide love or a reasonable facsimile of it. If there were more love, there would be less poverty, hunger, homelessness, and crime.

"What's love got to do with it?" you might ask. What's love got to do with meeting the needs of the people of the world? What's love got to do with changing the tragic and troubled climate of our world, of our lives and the lives of people around us?

Some of us ask that kind of question because we don't yet understand the true nature and power of love. We have a distorted or false image of what real love is.

Some of us continue to believe that love is the fluttery feeling like butterflies flying around in your stomach as you await the arrival of that special someone. That's not love, that's anticipation!

Others of us think of love as the sweet sensation that you feel when you're anywhere near your beloved or when he or she looks at you. That's not love either, that's infatuation. Love is not just hugs and kisses, the emotional becoming physical; that's affection.

On the other hand, love is not the giving or taking of emotional or physical abuse. That's definitely a distortion. Love at its best is not the syrupy, the sweet, the emotional, the special feelings that often abruptly come and go. Love is not just a secondhand emotion.

Actually, the sign and symbol of real love, as it is made clear to us in the scriptures, is not sweet by the world's standards. For the sign of real love is the cross of Calvary and the death of Christ Jesus.

To some, the death of Christ was simply the result of the Pharisees' political ploy to rid themselves and the world of an agitator, one who was robbing them of their attention and authority among the people. To others the death of Jesus may appear to be just the senseless murder of an innocent man.

There are others who would agree that the death of Christ is the symbol of shame and reproach. But I submit to you that the death of Jesus was more than simply a political ploy; it was more than just the execution of an innocent man. The death of Jesus *was* a symbol of shame and reproach, but it was more than that. The death of Jesus was the ultimate expression of God's love for humankind.

Paul says in Romans 5:8, "God proves his love for us in that while we still were sinners Christ died for us."

In the death of Christ on Calvary, the love of God is made clear. One songwriter said:

> God proved his love on Calvary
> when he gave his only Son to die for you and me.
> And the Bible tells the story
> How Jesus left his glory to come to earth
> by virgin birth and die.
> Look at the cross and see him there.
> See his bleeding hands, his side, his feet and
> the crown he wears. If you wonder why he came to die
> in bitter agony,
> Well, God proved his love on Calvary.

God is love. The love of God reveals God's nature and character. Everything we want to know about real love is found in the expression of God's love for us through the death of Christ on Calvary.

First John 3:16 says, "We know love by this, that he laid down his life for us."

Paul makes it clear in this evening's text the nature of real love as well as the depth, the full extent of God's love for us.

If only you knew how much God loves you. If only you could comprehend the magnitude of God's love for you as you sit there in your cold, dark, and bitter little world feeling unloved and unlovable, the sun would begin to shine for you and your life would begin to take on a whole new dimension and perspective. I can hear some of you saying, "What's love got to do with it?" What's love got to do with the state of my head and heart?

Let me try to make it plain for you. Paul says:

> For while we were still weak, at the right time Christ died for the ungodly. Indeed, rarely will anyone die for a righteous person—though perhaps for a good person someone might actually dare to die. But God proves his love for us in that while we still were sinners Christ died for us.

Paul says when we were powerless, the King James Version says when we were "without strength," when we were helpless, incapable of doing the right thing, of doing what is right, paying for our guilt and throwing off the miserable bondage to sin we found ourselves in, Christ died for us. We were sinners. I know you don't like hearing that but it's the truth. We ought to admit it, like the little girl who kept getting into trouble and getting spanked by her mother. Each time her mother spanked her, she promised to be good. But then she would mess up again. Finally her mother said to her, "Honey, I don't like spanking you. You promised me that you would be good." Honey said, "I'm trying to be good. But I guess it's just not my nature to be good." Paul said it this way, "The good that I would is not what I do, but what I hate to do."

We were powerless, helpless—nothing that we could do was sufficient to meet our moral need or satisfy the emptiness that was inside us or any of the other needs that we had.

We were sinners, alienated from God because of our sin, cut off from God because God hates sin and can't stand to have it in his presence.

To make matters worse, Paul says that we were ungodly; not only were we alienated from God because of the presence of sin in our lives, but there was nothing in our moral character that even remotely linked us to God. "Even our righteousness was as filthy rags."

One would think that God who is all holy and good, God who is light and in him is not even the slightest hint of darkness, God who is just and fair in all his dealings, could have easily, in all fairness, allowed the consequences of our sin to take its course, leaving us to continue to live in our miserable state and die in it. But he did not. He could not. God loves us, and because he loves us, he looked beyond our faults and saw our need. He provided for us when our need was the greatest. He did for us what we could not do for ourselves. When we could see no way, God made a way for us out of no way. He always does. God specializes in impossible situations. Impossibilities for humans are possibilities and opportunities for God to respond to our need. That's love!

You see, at just the right time, when we were powerless, when our need was greatest, Christ died for us. At just the right time! The death of Christ was not an accident of history, it was a powerful act of God. God carefully chose the time to send Jesus into the world born of a woman, and God also chose the time for him to die. God chose the time to perform this act of love to get the maximum benefit out of it. God's timing was not meant to primarily correspond to the political, religious, or social climate; God's timing was to correspond to our need.

God's always there when we need him. Always there, right on time, responding to your need. That's love!

The love of God is sacrificial. It is self-giving. God was in Christ. There was a relationship between them of the most intimate kind. God loved—Christ died. God gave his best to us. Nothing secondhand, picked over, leftover, messed over, refused. God gave us God's best. God gave God's self. What more could God give, and God gave his best for those who did not merit, deserve, were not worthy of his love.

That's what makes the love of God so powerful. Not only did God do for us what we could not do for ourselves, but God did for us what we probably would not even be willing to do for another.

Paul makes this point by saying, "Very rarely will anyone die for a righteous person." The righteous persons that he is referring to here are the kinds of persons who follow the letter of the law so perfectly that they turn people off with their holier-than-thou attitude. Righteous persons aren't concerned about people's feelings. Their only concern is dotting every "i" and crossing every "t." Even though they appear worthy, no one would die for them.

But the good persons, the ones who do not lack righteousness but are at least kind and giving to others: someone might dare to die for them.

But let's be honest, do you know anyone *you would be willing to die for*?

The question for us would be: is that person worthy of the sacrifice I would have to make? Do they deserve my love? Notice that God did not even consider our worthiness for the sacrifice of his Son. God knew that we weren't worthy!

Dare we ask what love's got to do with the death of Christ on Calvary? Love is unconditional. It gives without concern for the other's worth or worthiness. It accepts persons where they are and lifts them to where they ought to be. Love is forgiving, it is redeeming, it is reconciling.

Love is understanding. It is sensitive to where another person is. Love is willing to go to where they are. Love places itself in the other person's place.

Four times in three verses, Paul records the phrase "to die for." In each instance the preposition that is used means "on behalf of," to express the substitutionary nature of the sacrifice of Christ. But it also is to express the event of death on behalf of another because of the loving empathy of God.

Jesus died for us at Calvary, he died in our place on our behalf. He did it to express God's loving empathy for us. To be empathetic is to enter the world of other people. To be empathetic is to somehow get under their skin. To know not only what they are thinking but what they are feeling and experiencing, so that you can somehow feel and experience it with them.

When Jesus came to earth, he left his home in glory. He left his place and came to earth. He took off his robe of glory and got under our skin. He took on our humanity. He became like us.

Jesus knows all about us. He knows the good and the bad we've done. He knows our every weakness and the battles that we have won. He knows when we are tempted, and he knew just what to do. We had a debt we could not pay; he paid a debt he did not owe. Jesus paid it all, all to him I owe, sin had left a crimson stain. He washed it white as snow. He did it because he loves us. I've never known love like this before.

What's love got to do with it? Because God loves us, in the death of Christ on Calvary he has responded to our need. When we confess Jesus Christ as our Savior, we are forgiven of our sins. And though we keep on sinning, the promise is given. If we confess our sins, God is faithful and just to forgive us and to cleanse us from all unrighteousness. That's love.

And he just keeps on loving us, and being there for us, caring about us, seeing us through the good times and the bad. That's love.

That other stuff may be sweet, but this is sweeter. I've never known love like this before. How about you? What's love got to do with the troubled and tragic condition of our world?

There's a world of people out there who are in need of love. Everybody needs love. Their needs must be responded to. They need to be cared for, accepted, forgiven, healed, reconciled, talked to, listened to, hugged, held. Some folks just need to be acknowledged. Their needs aren't any different from ours.

As representatives of Christ, we who have come to know God's love need to let others know how sweet it is.

We need to love somebody like God loves us. We really don't have to go very far to begin to love folks. Start right here. In this very room, there are needs to be responded to, there are hurts that need healing, brokenness that needs mending. In this very room there is sin that needs forgiving by God and by you.

In this very room, there are persons who need to be encouraged and affirmed. Let's begin to love, really love one another here and then watch it grow and spread beyond this room into all the world.

Marking Time

John Tunstall

John Tunstall is founding pastor of Abundant Life Christian Church in Los Angeles, California. John graduated from Butler University and studied at Christian Theological Seminary. This sermon was preached at the tenth biennial National Convocation of the Christian Church.

Joshua 3

Well, it'll help if you turn to the book of Joshua. The book of Joshua, chapter three. The last three days we have been pricked by the theme of this Convocation, "Chosen by the Spirit and Challenged to Be." Now, I don't know about you, but for the last three days I've been trying to figure out: challenged to be *what*? I mean, what are we gonna do when we leave here Saturday? Well, I hope that when we leave here, we will be challenged to be God-directed, anointed, unctionized, energized soldiers! I mean, you ought to go home a little bit different than when you came here. The songwriter said, "We are watch soldiers." In the army, we are what? Soldiers. Take somebody by the hand and say, "Neighbor, I'm glad I'm a soldier." We are soldiers in the army. Where you going, soldier? Somebody said, "We're marching to Zion." For this we've been challenged to be. Have we been challenged to be a better

124

equipped soldier? And if we are marching to Zion, I just came here tonight to share some *marching orders.*

I've always been fascinated with drill teams. As a matter of fact, when I was in school not too long ago, I was very impressed by the ROTC brothers and I was always impressed by the drill team brothers. And every time I got a chance to march, I just would suck up everything that I could suck up about marching, the drill team. I wanted to be a Marine, because at that time the Marines would come home from the service with those handsome dress blues on and they would seem to get all the pretty girls and I wanted to be a Marine to get to dress up in those dress blues and also just to learn how to march.

I remember just like it was yesterday when I was involved in drill team; I remember these four commands. And these four commands that I came by to share with you at this late-night session of the National Convocation—I believe that in these four commands, God epitomizes and God recapitulates what he wants us to do when we leave here. Four commands.

Number one: I remember that before marching began, there was always the command "Fall in." Fall in! It didn't matter what you had been doing, marching always began with "fall in." I mean you can just be laying back, playing cool and the drill sergeant shouts "fall in" and you shove off and you just start marching. "Fall in!" You jump up and just start marching. You have to stop doing whatever you've been doing whenever you heard the command, "fall in." The second command was "Attention." Attention! Att-tennn-tion! And "attention" means to give immediate focus.

Then there was a third command and this third command was "Mark time." Mark time. And when you're marking time you're just marching in place, not going nowhere. Not going forwards, not going backwards, but you're just marking time. And there was always some good news about the command to "mark time" because the command that always followed "mark time" was the command "Forward, march!" Forward march.

That's what I want to talk about tonight. For I also see Joshua giving these same four commands to God's people. I hear God telling Joshua, "Joshua, you tell my people first of all to 'Fall in,' then you tell them 'Attention,' 'Mark time,' and 'Forward march.'"

Now for some brief biblical historicity of this text here in Joshua, chapter three. Here we find God's chosen people at camp, on the far side of the Jordan River. They camped right there on the creek bank of the Jordan River. On their side of the river was the wilderness, and on the other side of the river there was Canaan—this land that was flowing with milk and honey, this promised land. And here I see, in verse two of this third chapter, it came to pass that after three days God instructed the officers to go through the camp and issue these commands: "All right now, fall in!" Fall in! The leadership said, "You've been wandering long enough, now fall in." And "fall in" means that you've been doing what you've been doing long enough. Now it's time to "fall in."

You know something, brothers and sisters, I believe that God is saying to some of us here tonight, right here at this National Convocation, I believe that God is telling some of us to "fall in." God is saying to some of us, "You've been praying that same old prayer long enough, now 'fall in.'" God is saying, "You've been reading that same one scripture verse now, oh, for forty-two years, now 'fall in.'" You've been sitting on this same pew long enough, now God is saying, "fall in." You've been seeking that same blessing long enough, you've been naming and praying it long enough, now God is saying, "I want you to 'fall in.'" You've been asking for forgiveness for that same old nickel-and-dime sin long enough, God is saying, "Fall in." You've been falling in that same ditch long enough, God is saying, "Fall in." You've been doing whatever you've been doing long enough, God is saying, "Fall in." "Fall in!" "Fall in."

Somebody said, "Well, pastor, what happens when I 'fall in'?" Look here at verse fourteen. And it came to pass, "When the people set out from their tents...." When the people set out from their tents...when the people set out from their tents.... "Reverend, how come you keep saying that over and over again?" Because there's something about setting out from their tents. "Well, what's a tent?" Tents, in this context, represent temporary comfort. A tent is a dwelling place that was not meant to be permanent. And when these Israelites, when they moved from one place to another place, they pitched their tents, and when it was time for them to move on, then they would do what? They would pick up their tents and move on.

Now there may be some of us here tonight who have been walking around in our own personal tents for too long. It could be that there are some of us here tonight who have been living in our own personal comfort zone too long, and God wants us to pick up our tents and set out from our tents and move on. Some of our tents could be pet sins. It could be that God wants us to fall in and move out from our tents. Some tents could be relationships that we have no business dibbling and dabbling in. And God is telling somebody here tonight to "fall in." I hear God say to somebody, "I want to bless you, but I want you to fall in. I want to build you up but I want you to fall in. I want you to have heaven on earth but you must fall in. I want you to have abundant life that Jesus came to give us but he wants us to fall in. God said, "I want to lift you, I want to deliver you, I want to heal you, I want to fill you with the Holy Ghost, but you must fall in!" Fall in. Fall in.

But I also hear Joshua saying something else. Chapter three, verse three: The officers "commanded the people, 'When you see the ark of the covenant of the LORD your God being carried by the levitical priests, then you shall set out from your place. Follow it." Go after it. When you see the ark, set out from your place and go after it. I hear God saying, "Attention." God said, "Focus your attention on that ark."

Now some of us remember the biblical significance of the ark of the covenant. The contents of that chest were believed to be the very presence and the power of God. And God instructed the leadership, "Don't allow folk to dibble and dabble and mess with that ark. Don't allow folk to look at it, don't allow folk to touch it," but they were supposed to demand the utmost of *attention*. Don't get too close to it, but just focus your attention on the ark. And here the man of God is saying, "When the ark moves, you move."

You remember in that movie that was out a few years ago, *Indiana Jones and the Raiders of the Lost Ark*, when they opened up the ark all kinds of stuff started happening. I mean stuff started flying around and weird noises erupted from the earth, when they opened up that ark. But here the man of God is telling the people, focus your *attention* on that ark. He's saying, "Make the power and the presence of God the priority of your *attention*." God wants us today to make the presence of himself and his omnipotence the focus of our *attention*.

And remember that when the Israelites would camp they would always put the ark in the middle of the camp, and then the tribes would encamp around it. But here in this text, as

God prepares to lead the people to victory, instead of the ark being in the center of the camp, now God wants the people to put the ark at the *head* of the camp.

In other words, it could be that God wants to do more with us if we would get beyond just being satisfied with having Jesus in our lives, but it could be that God wants the Holy Ghost to have priority over our lives. It could be that many of us are content with the Holy Spirit as being resident, but he wants to be president. He wants to do more than reside, but it could be that he wants to *preside*. But in order for God to do that, we must focus. Gods wants our attention. God is telling some of us here tonight, "Fall in!" God is telling some of us here tonight, "Attention!"

But then too, I see here something else. I see here in verse fourteen, "When the people set out from their tents to cross over the Jordan, the priests bearing the ark of the covenant were in front of the people." Here we see the priests, the men of God, in front of the people carrying this ark. We see the preachers in front of the people bearing the presence and the power of God. And here we see these preachers now, here we see them at this Jordan River, at a particular time of year when the Jordan River was overflowing. One scholar says,"It became as the snow had melted in the mountains and it had rushed down and the Jordan River was flowing at a pace of forty or fifty miles per hour." That made it impossible from a human standpoint for anybody to cross the river.

The Word of God says that the priests were carrying this ark and now the preachers know that if they do not go into the water, the people cannot pass through the water. But when we see these preachers carrying the ark of the covenant, the questions comes to mind: What are the people doing? What's the congregation doing? What's the fellowship doing? Here we've got the men of God out front carrying the ark, but what's the congregation doing? Here we see the preachers now at this water carrying this ark and God tells them, "Preachers, if you just dip your feet into the water...." God said that he was gonna heap the waters up on both sides, but while God was still dealing with the preachers, what are the people doing? Marking time. Just marking time. Going nowhere. There's our bunch, just marking time. The people couldn't go forward, they couldn't go backward, but all they were doing was marking time.

Have you ever felt that way, as if God has maybe put you in neutral? I mean, put you on hold or something? You can't go forward. You can't go backward. I believe there's some folk here tonight who know something about that. You know something about what it is to spend some lonely hours. You had to mark time. You know what it is for the devil to dig ditches in front of you and all you could do was mark time. Somebody here tonight, you know what it is for the devil to have ripped off your finances and all you could do was mark time. The devil has torn up your family and all you can do is mark time. Damaged your health and all you can do is mark time. The devil turns the folk against you, even in your own church, and all you can do is mark time. You confuse your mind and all you can do is mark time. *Mark time. Mark time.* You know all the biblical promises but all you can do is mark time.

There's a theological word for this *marking time* and it's called *transcendence*, and this word *transcendence* means "the turning point"—the in-between time, the in-the-meantime, the time between being sick and being healed. But that meantime, that in-between time, that time between you and your sweetie pie fussing and fighting and the kiss-and-make-up time: what about that? The meantime, when all we can do is mark time. Just mark time.

I just came by tonight to say that there is some good news about *marking time*. I remember that there's only one command that could follow *mark time*. I remember those cold days in Indiana when I was in drill team and we'd be outside, fifteen to twenty below zero, just marking time. Oh, we'd be outside in the snow and my feet'd be so cold, hands be so numb, but we just say, *mark time. Mark time. Mark time.* And sometimes you almost have to force yourself to *mark time*. But I remember the good news, there's always one command that followed *mark time* and we always looked forward to it and that command was always, "Forward, march." *Forward, march.*

And here we see all the old men of God with their feet in the water, and God rolling back the waters on the left and rolling back the waters on the right and here was God who made a highway through a waterway and then who says, "All right, folks, now we've been marking time long enough, so come on now. We're gonna cross to the other side of Canaan now. Come on now. *Forward, march! Forward, march!*" And I believe, oh, I believe, that God is telling that to some of us here tonight. He wants us to go back to Indianapolis, he wants us to go back to Alabama. He wants us to go back to California, and Nashville, and *forward, march. Forward, march.*

Well, as I take my seat let me just call forth a few others of God's soldiers who knew what it was to have been marking time and then God said, "Forward, march." Remember Moses at the Red Sea, Pharaoh's army behind him—oh, yes, on one side was a mountain range and the other side was a mountain range and right in front was nothing but the sea. But then God told the man of God, "Stretch forth your rod" and the waters parted. And once the waters parted, Moses looked back and said, "All right, folks, go on now: *Forward, march.*"

Remember in the book of Daniel, how King Nebuchadnezzar took brother Shadrach and brother Meshach and brother Abednego and just threw them in that fiery furnace, oh, yes, and he looked in and he saw those three boys just walking around, he saw them in the furnace marking time. They were just sitting in there marking time, until God said, "All right now, I want you all to come out now," and God said, "All right now, *forward, march.*" Out came Shadrach. Out came Meshach. Out came Abednego. But wait a minute. We only threw three in; who's that fourth fellow? He looks like the Son of God. *Forward, march.*

Jesus himself was a soldier. He was a soldier. Oh, they marched him into the courtroom, they marched him before Pilate, they marched him to the killing ground. Oh, they nailed him to an old rugged cross, where they put a nail in his left hand, a nail in his right hand, they put a crown of thorns on his head, they pierced him in his side. The Bible says that on that Friday, he died. Oh yes, he died. Then came Friday night, and he was doing nothing but marking time. Saturday morning Jesus was doing nothing but *marking time.* Saturday afternoon Jesus was doing nothing but *marking time.* Saturday night he was doing nothing but *marking time.* But early Sunday morning, early Sunday morning, God dispatched an angel and God said, "All right now, you've been marking time long enough, now *forward, march. Forward, march. Forward, march.*"

I'm so glad about Jesus. I've got the marching orders tonight and I'm go glad there ain't nobody, nobody, nobody, who treats me like Jesus 'cause he's my friend. Well, somebody says, "Reverend, how do you spell relief? R-o-l-a-i-d-s?"

No, no, no! I spell it J-E-S-U-S! J—means that I'm justified. E—means that I'm edified. S—means that I'm sanctified. U—means that I'm unified. S—means that I'm satisfied. No, nobody treats me like Jesus.

I've got some marching orders and I thank the Lord for that. *Fall in.* You've been doing what you've been doing long enough. Fall in. *Attention.* God wants our attention. Undivided attention. Don't worry about marking time. Don't worry about it, just keep on *marking time,* don't give up. And always, after you mark time, comes the command to *forward, march!*

There may be somebody here tonight, as a delegate to this National Convocation, but if the truth were told you're not really saved, you've never fallen in. You've been playing the game, a lot of folks think you're saved, but you need to fall in. Fall in. Salvation is possible for you tonight. *Fall in. Give God your attention, your undivided attention.* And some of us here tonight may say, "Well, Pastor, I'm already saved, but I've been blowing it. I've been playing church. I've not been giving God top priority—I've been *marking time.* I want to recommit my life back to the Lord. When I go back home, when the benediction is over at this Convocation, I want to be a powerful soldier for the Lord." Well, then, listen to what God is saying to you: "*Fall in. Attention.* The time for *marking time* is over. I want you to *forward, march!*"

$\mathscr{B}$eing Comfortable with Uncomfortableness

Floyd Knight, Jr.

Floyd Knight served most recently as associate pastor of First Christian Church in Blue Springs, Missouri. A graduate of Indiana University and Boston University, he has done doctoral studies at the University of Chicago in the area of Hebrew Bible. An accomplished musician, Floyd also serves on the hymnal development committee for the forthcoming *Chalice Hymnal.*

1 Corinthians 9:19–23

Several years ago, I discovered a truth that was and is universal. I discovered what Thomas Wolfe, the famous American writer, discovered in 1938—that *you can't go home again.* In his novel by that name, Wolfe explores how growth and development from childhood to adolescence to adulthood affects our understanding of home. Although one may return to one's place of birth, one could never return to one's youthful innocence and ignorance. As a child we could dream dreams and see the world as complete and whole and utterly safe. As a child we felt invincible and safe from harm. The arms of our saviors were real and were made of flesh and blood. We had only to cry for momma or daddy, and we would be delivered from harm and protected from all unhappiness.

Doug Ramsey wrote in a letter to a friend that "Wolfe listed all the things to which you can't go home again, from

132

family to dreams...and concluded that 'although you can't go home again, the home of every one of us is in the future: there is no other way.'"

Simply put, several years ago I discovered that home was no longer home, that the home of my childhood, of my youth, and of my early adulthood was forever in the past. It made no difference that my father and mother still lived in the same house, on the same block, in the same neighborhood. It made no difference that all the rooms and furnishings had remained the same. Psychologically, the home of my youth had become my father's and mother's home. I had become an adult who had his own home, own furnishings, and his own immediate family. The only place where I truly felt comfortable was the home of my own making. The home of my youth would now forever be my father's and mother's home.

I suspect that many of you who are married can very well recall your own experience of this discovery, of feeling strangely both at peace in and yet estranged from the home of your youth. I can recall how the bed and bedroom that I had thought were so comfortable before I left home were now too small and too confining whenever I came home to visit. I can recall how the universe of family, block, neighborhood, and church, which had seemed so infinite, were now finite and confining. Years later I learned to be comfortable with this uncomfortableness. I learned that although I could never go back to those enchanted days of my youth, I could nevertheless work for the enchantment of the future. Although Peter Pan had the option of not growing up, we aren't as fortunate. We all must learn to be comfortable with this uncomfor-tableness. We must all learn, like Thomas Wolfe, that comfort cannot be found in a retreat from the realities of this world, from the realities of change, decay, pain, evil, and responsibility. In an address given five months before he died, Wolfe said:

> I did not know that for [a person] who wants to continue with the creative life, [who wants] to keep on growing and developing, this cheerful idea of happy establishment, [that is] of continuing now as one has started, is nothing but a delusion and a snare. I did not know that if a man [or woman] really has in [them] the...power of further growth and further development, there can be no such thing as an easy road.... I did not know...that

with each new effort would come new desperation, the new, and old, sense...of realizing again that there is no help anywhere save the help and strength that one can find within him- [or her-] self.

What Wolfe looks for inside himself, we look to God, the author and finisher of our faith.

In our reading for the day, Paul writes to a congregation in the midst of turmoil, sectarian division, and strife. The church in Corinth had focused their attention on the perishable things of the Spirit and of the Christian life. They were not divided over truth versus error, over correct doctrine versus heresy. No, the Corinthians had focused their attention not on error and evil, but on the weapons that God had given them to battle the same. They fought over the gifts of the Spirit, over whether speaking in tongues, prophesying, healing and/or special knowledge was better or more desirable than the other. They fought over the visible, outward forms of saintliness instead of examining the inner motivations.

Paul, using his own life, calling, authority, and freedom in Christ, appeals to the strong, to the mature, to focus their minds on the nonperishable gifts of the Spirit—faith, hope, and love. If they would concentrate on these things, then the strife that they were experiencing would be no more. Those who are strong are those who not only have the knowledge of liberty to eat and to drink things sacrificed to idols, but who have the love to bear with the weak who have not as yet been so convicted:

> For though I am free with respect to all, I have made myself a slave to all, so that I might win more of them. To the Jews I became as a Jew, in order to win Jews. To those under the law I became as one under the law (though I myself am not under the law) so that I might win those under the law. To those outside the law I became as one outside the law (though I am not free from God's law but am under Christ's law) so that I might win those outside the law. To the weak I became weak, so that I might win the weak. I have become all things to all people, that I might by all means save some. I do it all for the sake of the gospel, so that I may share in its blessings.
>
> 1 Corinthians 9:19–23

Paul's response is grounded in the reality that it is God who decides what is ultimately of worth, what is one's labor, and what is one's wage in and among the church. As the psalmist said, the earth and the heavens and all that is in them are the Lord's. Servants of the king have no authority to decide either their own labor or their worth in the eyes of their king. They can only and should only seek to do what their Lord has appointed them to do. *Their own likes or dislikes, values and comfort cannot be forced on others, for the only values which are of importance are those of the Lord.* In many ways, the Corinthians were like sons and daughters who would deny the rights of their parents to be lord of their own home. The Corinthians were like sons and daughters living in their father's house and all the while striving and contending with one another over who would lord it over the other and, therefore, have the right to dwell in comfort. They are like silly children who failed to realize that there can be only one lord and one mistress in each house while the parents are still alive.

When we argue over liturgy or fight over styles of music, are we not like the Corinthians—are we not like sons and daughters who would deny God's right to be lord of God's own home? Are we not like disobedient children each seeking to set the rules and lord it over the others just to maximize our own personal comfort and to exercise our own will despite the wish of our parents that we should all dwell in peace?

When we as the church are more concerned with what we like over what will bring others to Christ, haven't we become like the Corinthians? Haven't we also failed to realize that we are only workers in the Kingdom, and not its Lord, and that the church is the house of God, established by the blood of Christ, not the blood and sweat of our own brow?

We have no right to seek our own comfort and desires. We have no right to say what can or can't be done. We have no right as mature Christians to not change if change will save some. We are called to be all things to all people so that by all means we may save some, not just the means that you or I are most comfortable with or most familiar with or prefer.

God has called us to a life of discomfort. God has called us to be sojourners in a land not our own. We are called to empty ourselves as Christ emptied himself, having taken on the form of humanity, humbling himself to take on the stigma of sin so that we all might be reconciled to God. Christ left the comfort of heaven, not to bring us comfort in this world, but inner peace.

> Do not think that I have come to bring peace to the earth;
> I have not come to bring peace, but a sword.
>> For I have come to set a man against his father,
>> and a daughter against her mother,
>> and a daughter-in-law against her mother-in-law;
>> and one's foes will be members of ones own house-
>>   hold....
> Whoever does not take up the cross and follow me is not worthy of me. Those who find their life will lose it, and those who lose their life for my sake will find it.
>
> Matthew 10:34–36, 38–39

You don't like the new hymns. You aren't comfortable with that preaching style. You don't like the clapping. You are not comfortable with that type of singing and shouting. You aren't familiar with that new liturgy. You get confused with changes. You, you, you, and yours. Have you not forgotten the reason why you were called? To go make disciples. You were called to take up your cross even if your own family would disown you, even if it meant being persecuted and talked about and hated, even if it meant being homeless, naked, and hungry. When your own comfort takes precedence over reaching those for whom Christ died, you run the risk of losing your own life and salvation. When your own comfort takes precedence over reaching those for whom Christ died, you turn the gospel of service into a Bill of Rights for your comfort. But God did not call us into comfort, but into service.

> You know that among the Gentiles those whom they recognize as their rulers lord it over them, and their great ones are tyrants over them. But it is not so among you; but whoever wishes to become great among you must be your servant, and whoever wishes to be first among you must be slave of all. For the Son of Man came not to be served but to serve, and to give his life a ransom for many."
>
> Mark 10:42a–45

Why should we care whether this saint or that saint would feel upset or uncomfortable with introducing this song or that liturgy into our service of worship if it will bring men and women to Christ? I care about correct doctrine. I care about presenting the word of God undefiled. But why should we care more about our comfort, our wants, our traditions when there are people out there who need the love of God, who need salvation, who need hope, love, and forgiveness?

We are called to be all things to all people so that we may by all means save some. We were not called to be all things to some people—those who think like us, who vote like us, who worship and walk, talk, and speak like us. We were called to be all things to all people—Black, Hispanic, Native American, and Asian.

We were called to be all things to all people so that by all means, we might save some. By all means, not just those you and I are most comfortable with or are most familiar with. But by all means so that the Greek and the Jew, the European and the African, those who speak English and those who do not, those who are White and aged and those who are of color and young may find salvation. We must never confuse spiritual comfort with our own physical, cultural, and emotional comfort. The comfort of humanity is fleeting, but there is a joy and a comfort and a peace that passes all understanding. Let us not confuse God's gift with our own selfishness.

I began this sermon by speaking about my feeling of being comfortable with uncomfortableness. I spoke about how I no longer felt at home in my father's and mother's house, about how I no longer felt as comfortable at their home as I do at my own. So too is it in the spiritual realm. The worship of our yesteryears must now undergo a similar development of perspective and will.

If we truly believe that God is our mother and our father, that God is the Lord of the earth and all that is on it, the sea and all that is in it, that we have a home from whence we shall no longer roam, and that we are not our own, but have been bought with a price, why do we behave as if the criterion of our own comfortableness applies to our churches?

When we visit our mother's home, we do not expect it to be as comfortable as our own home. In fact, we are comfortable with this uncomfortableness. We are comfortable despite the fact that the bed we sleep on is not as comfortable as the one in our own house or the fact that the bathroom of our youth has somehow become strange and somewhat unfamiliar. But yet when it comes to God's church, anything that is new or novel or different is quickly frowned upon.

The Scriptures say sing to the Lord a new song, but not in your congregation. The Scriptures record that on the day of Pentecost, the church was filled with the tongues of many nations, but in your church English only is the cry! Urban vernacular, Spanish, French, etc., are forbidden.

Revelation 7 tells us that there will be a great multitude dressed in white from every nation, tribe, people, and language. Paul, a Jew, wrote in Greek, not Aramaic. Our Bible, which was written in Greek, Aramaic, and Hebrew is now read by you in English. But yet you insist on being "Burger King," in having it "your way" instead of Christ's way.

Why is it that when it comes to God's home, we argue for our comfort instead of striving for the comfort that comes from God and the salvation of those who are lost? Have we come to think of our churches as being our own home instead of being God's?

If our parents have the right to make up the rules in their own home, why do we deny God the right to make up the rules which should govern God's church? If we respect the rights of our parents while we are in their home, why do we not respect the right of God to be worshiped in any way God so chooses? Does not our God have the same right in God's own house as our parents have in theirs? Do we have a right to expect God to cater to our own wants and comforts to the exclusion of those of our fellow brothers and sisters?

It is written that Christ,

> though he was in the form of God,
>> did not regard equality with God
>> as something to be exploited,
> but emptied himself,
>> taking the form of a slave,
>> being born in human likeness.
> And being found in human form,
>> he humbled himself
>> and became obedient to the point of death—
>> even death on a cross.
>
> Philippians 2:6–8

This is love and the way of love, a love which acts despite and in spite of the discomforts of life.

We are called to be slaves to one another, not lords. You say you want to reach out to the community, then become like the community so that you can employ all the means at your disposal to save some of them. This is not an option, it is God's commandment. You are called to be a slave of Christ Jesus, to serve others and not yourselves. If you are unable to suffer discomfort so that others may be saved, you will have no share in the kingdom.

How can I say this? First Corinthians 9:23 tells us why Paul tries to be all things to all people for the sake of the gospel and so that he might become a fellow partaker of it. There is a causal effect here. Paul becomes all things *so that he might become a fellow partaker* of the gospel. To become a fellow partaker of the gospel requires you to become like Christ and to forsake your comfort for the salvation of others. To put it bluntly, let me quote Jesus from Matthew again:

Whoever does not take up the cross and follow me is not worthy of me. Those who find their life will lose it, and those who lose their life for my sake will find it.

Matthew 10:38–39

Check your salvation! Whenever you and your leaders refuse to change, to become all things to all, because you aren't comfortable, simply because you didn't grow up with that type of worship, with that type of prayer, with that type of song or with that type of response, check your salvation. Whenever you and your leaders refuse to sponsor a Hispanic outreach program simply because you aren't comfortable, simply because you didn't grow up speaking or singing in Spanish, check your salvation. When you refuse to use all the means at your disposal simply because you weren't raised as an African American, a Latino American or an Asian American, check your salvation!

Condemnation comes because we put our personal comforts and wants above the gospel of Jesus Christ. Condemnation comes whenever our love flows only inward, instead of also outward to the world. If we truly loved Christ we would do the things of Christ.

Paul writes in another letter that

I have learned to be content with whatever I have. I know what it is to have little, and I know what it is to have plenty. In any and all circumstances I have learned the secret of being well-fed and of going hungry, of having plenty and of being in need. I can do all things through him who strengthens me.

Philippians 4:11a–13

Paul learned to be comfortable in uncomfortableness. He learned to follow Christ.

Jesus, who was of heaven, took on the form of humanity in order to save us. Paul, who was born a Jew—an African, took on the customs of the Europeans in order to save some. Are we who were born before the forties willing to be all things to those born after the fifties? I would check my salvation.

God has called us to be comfortable with uncomfortableness, to be content in whatever circumstances we find ourselves. I pray that you and I may find the power to be comfortable with uncomfortableness.

I leave you this morning with this thought, that the comfort we seek is not only in the future but also within us, for we have the Spirit of God. Go in grace, go in peace, go with comfort in discomfort until the world is no more. Amen.

*T*he Work of Ministry

Raymond E. Brown

Raymond E. Brown is a longtime Disciples pastor (at Willow Street Christian Church in Hannibal, Missouri) who is now retired and living in Indianapolis, Indiana. Ray graduated from Jarvis Christian College and attended Drake University School of Religion. He also served as executive vice-president of the Board of Church Extension of the Christian Church (Disciples of Christ).

Luke 9:57–62; Proverbs 4:1–4*

Hear, ye children, the instruction of a father, and attend to know understanding. For I give you good doctrine, forsake ye not my law. For I was my father's son, tender and only beloved in the sight of my mother. He taught me also, and said unto me, Let thine heart retain my words: keep my commandments, and live.

Proverbs 4:1–4

The ordination of a minister is one of the most significant events in the life of the church. For the minister it is a once-in-a-lifetime experience as by prayer and the traditional laying on of hands he or she is set apart to the work of his or her calling.

---

*The scripture references in this sermon are from the King James Version of the Bible.

It is an unusual event for the particular congregation as well. Any given congregation can expect to be host to this kind of service only two or three times in a generation. Unfortunately, some congregations have never been host to such a service. So this is a glorious day, a day of celebration, a day of commitment, a day of acceptance of a task. In any church the event is sufficiently unusual to invite attention to the work of ministry.

You are *called* to the work of ministry. You don't hear much about the call to ministry these days. There are those who consider the ministry because they feel it's a good profession, a respectable white-collar job. There are those who consider the ministry to be a good opportunity to acquire prestige, power, or advancement, or who consider it because of pressure from their parents, their pastor, or their friends. But the church still believes in a call from on high as personified by the prophet Isaiah as he describes his experiences:

> In the year that King Uzziah died I saw also the Lord sitting upon a throne, high and lifted up, and his train filled the temple. Above it stood the seraphims: each one had six wings; with two he covered his face, and with two he covered his feet, and with two he did fly. And one cried unto another and said, Holy, holy, holy is the LORD of hosts: the whole earth is full of his glory. And the posts of the door moved at the voice of him that cried, and the house was filled with smoke. Then said I, Woe is me! for I am undone; because I am a man of unclean lips, and I dwell in the midst of a people of unclean lips: for mine eyes have seen the King, the LORD of hosts. Then flew one of the seraphims unto me, having a live coal in his hand, which he had taken with the tongs from off the altar: And he laid it upon my mouth, and said, Lo, this hath touched thy lips; and thine iniquity is taken away, and thy sin purged. Also I heard the voice of the Lord, saying, Whom shall I send, and who will go for us? Then said I, Here am I; send me!"

Strip away the imagery and these words containing the prophet's call are intensely practical. They give the keynote of his life, and sum up in a few striking sentences the spirit and purpose of his ministry.

The call to ministry begins with a confrontation between God and the individual. No matter how you cut it, you must be called by God. There is nothing necessarily mystical about it, even though Isaiah saw a vision and heard a voice, and Paul was confronted with a presence and had speech with the living Christ. Such instances of an encounter with God have marked the call of thousands to the service of Christ, and though I grew up in a culture where this type of experience was the test of the validity of the call, I firmly believe that those are not to be taken as the norm but are special cases and generally occur when there is a sudden change in the direction which the life must take. I have come to believe, based upon the experiences of others as well as my own, that in more instances the call comes as the result of a growing awareness of what one may and ought to do with his or her life. But make no mistake, whether suddenly and dramatically or slowly and progressively, ministry begins with God's call. "You are called" means that God has already and explicitly asked you to enter his service. Isaiah saw the Lord. Each person who is called sees the Lord. Whether with the naked eye, with the mind's eye, or in a vision, it is what a person sees that makes or unmakes that person; and Isaiah saw the Lord, himself, and his duty.

In twentieth-century America, how does God call persons to ministry? The traditional working of the call may be like that of Isaiah or of Levi—a simple "follow me." And God has a purpose in the call. God wants persons for a life of fellowship and service in the world. God does not call us to escape from the world, much less to turn our backs upon it and pretend it is not there. The God who reveals himself in and through the events recorded in the Bible is the Lord of history, infinitely concerned not only with women and men who are in the world but also with the whole of life and every area of it. You are called so that God's love, mercy, justice, and joy may permeate and change industry, politics, family, and community life, as well as individual men and women.

Behind every great statesman, or reformer, whether that person speaks our theological dialect or not, is a vision of the power that leads the universe and every atom of it to lofty ends, whose forces run everywhere, and whose energies are more than we see and hear and know—the Lord of hosts. A person may not intelligently believe all the truth about the experiences of Isaiah, but if that person is to organize society and guide people well, if that person is to reform abuses and reconstitute broken-down humanity, that person must, with the inner eye of thought and faith, see that the powers above life are supreme over those beneath it, that there are more and finer energies in the unseen than the seen. The call to ministry comes—it comes to each of us personally, yet we may hear it differently.

I believe that God calls us indirectly through others. The minister stands in the pulpit speaking of the critical leadership needs throughout the world. You begin to think of someone who might be just the person until someone directs the question to you. Then you're upset. That wasn't what you intended at all.

Many of us heard it first as a call from below, the cry of human need. There is the cry which comes swelling up from the poor, the dispossessed, the powerless, from those in doubt, those in trouble, those struggling with daily temptations, the illiterate, the sick, the orphans, the homeless. We heard it in the cry of a child hungering for bread, or possibly a youth in the throes of need for a fix, or in a church starving for spiritual leadership. Moses, among the sheep of his father-in-law, in the faraway wilderness of Horeb, still could not forget the voices of his people, until finally one day through them he heard the voice of God, "I have seen the affliction of my people. I know their sufferings, and I have come down to deliver them. Come, I will send you." All those conspicuously called in the Bible were called in relationship to the affliction of their people. Why, then, should the call be different for you? And why should we think the answer was any easier for them?

This human cry is often a challenge to God. But it is really God's challenge to us. God has been preparing his answer. Just as, in the hidden laboratory of nature, coal has been prepared for the world's need of warmth; just as, nursed in secret stores, electricity has been prepared for the world's need of light and speed; just as, in the slow working of history, the fundamental answer to all problems was prepared in the Incarnation, so year after year, by quiet influences, by teaching, by a mother's prayers, by sermons, by an education, God has been slowly preparing his answer to this cry, and *you* are that answer.

So when the cry from below is heard, the ears open to the call from above. Then the human cry becomes more articulate and insistent. Moses heard the cry of his people, and struck a blow for them. But at the first sign of danger, he fled. Then God came and sent him down into Egypt to deliver them and he was no longer afraid of the wrath of the king.

Martin Luther King heard the cries of his people and the call from above which led him all the way from Montgomery to Memphis, consumed with a passion for bettering the people amongst whom he lived, and he laid down his life on their behalf!

God calls all persons into the church. You are not called in a general or abstract way, but into the church in order that you may fulfill your ministry, in order that you may grow to maturity, help other people to grow, and extend the opportunity to all people. You must never forget that God calls persons to serve the Christian community—the church. God calls at infinite pain to himself. God has a purpose in his call. It is God's plan, not yours. God calls you to serve his purposes, not yours!

When you begin to put all this together, some of us get real anxious when we recognize the dangers that are inherent in it. Therefore, I would like to remind you of this incident. A group of young men were walking on a country road near town. They were engaged in a lively discussion with Jesus. It was probably the earliest reported dialogue on the nature of the ministry. Caught under the spell of Jesus, one young man in a burst of enthusiasm stated: "I'll follow you wherever you go." Jesus was no fool. He turned and stared at the young man, his eyes expressed disbelief. "Will you really?" he said. "Don't you know that foxes have holes and birds have nests, but I don't even have a place to sleep!"

The young man was lost for words—a highly unlikely situation for most clergy. How serious was the young man's intention? What game was being played between Jesus and this young man? Words, you know, come easily; they can be cheap and ineffectual. At times, our words outrun our convictions. Most of us, I suspect, suffer from a credibility gap in our relation with Jesus. Today we need to be aware of this credibility gap and be challenged to undergird our commitment to Christ.

Commitment is difficult to achieve for any disciple of Jesus Christ. To follow Jesus is no guarantee of anything, not even an adequate pension. Peter realized this when he denied Jesus. You cannot play it safe and follow Jesus. Yet many of us try to do both—play it safe and follow Christ.

But I'm here today to tell you that this calls on you to risk all that you are and have for the sake of the one who called.

But finally, let me tell you this. You are something special. Not because you are handsome. Not because you have an attractive wife. Not even because of anything you have done. But you are special. You are special because you come from some special people. Like the apostle Paul, I call to remembrance the faith that is in you, a faith that dwelt first in your father, and your mother. You're something special. You come from a long line of persons whose hope is built on nothing less than Jesus' blood and righteousness.

You are something special because when Satan was on your trail so that the glitters of this world began to shut out for you the glories of our God, there were hundreds of persons who fell down on bony knees and prayed to God that you wouldn't get too far out there that you couldn't get back.

You are something special because you are a part of a community of faith that not only surrounded you with love and care and nurtured you in the fundamentals of the faith, but also developed educational institutions where training could take place and help develop within you some of the skills necessary to bring you to this time and place.

Yes, you are something special because of those who wore the chains, those forebears of yours who through toil, sweat, blood, and tears—who stepped back that you might go forward, who went hungry that you might eat, and sacrificed themselves that you might be free.

You are something special because there was one who came and walked the earth for a time, understood the faults and failures of ordinary people, who took on all the principalities and powers of this world and ended up out on a Judean hillside hanging from a cross because he believed that worth dying for and now is calling you to do his work.

And I charge you this day—don't you ever forget that you are something special. If you forget, may your tongue cleave to the roof of your mouth. If you forget, may your right hand wither! You are something special.

But don't let your pride get you down, but just know that you're something special so that you can hold your head high, throw your shoulders back, and never be ashamed that you answered the call; and every day you walk, walk in the spirit of the one who called you and said to you: "Don't worry, 'I'll be with you always even to the end of the age.'"

*T*he Minister's Credibility

Emmett Dickson

Emmett Dickson is a retired pastor, general staff executive, and college professor. A graduate of Southern Christian Institute in Edwards, Mississippi, and Butler University, Emmett served in leadership roles in the Christian Church for more than forty-four years. For twenty-five years he was the executive secretary of the National Christian Missionary Convention, the predecessor of the National Convocation of the Christian Church (Disciples of Christ). Upon his retirement in 1979, he was presented a certificate of distinguished service in the mission of the church by the Division of Homeland Ministries.

Matthew 9:37

Jesus said, "The harvest is plentiful, but the laborers are few" (Matthew 9:37). I'm talking about Christian ministry here. God calls us to ministry. But we have lost the mark. The credibility of the preacher has gone down. I tell you this morning, our credibility has gone down.

I was driving out of Texas the other day. I was driving a nice shiny car, had on my Johnson Stetson. I pulled in behind two state troopers and we were rolling on that ol' interstate up from Dallas into Arkansas. These two troopers were ahead of me in each car. As we drove along another one came in behind, and that put me in the triangle. We rode along like that for about twenty miles and then behind me became the signal of a different light—a flickity, flickity, flickiting. That meant for me to stop and pull over. So I did.

147

They came up to me and said, "May I have your operator's license?" I said, "Mister Officer, what is the difficulty?" He said, "You were exceeding the speed limit." I said, "Mister Officer, would you please offer another reason for stopping me? You saw the two cars ahead of me, didn't you?" He said, "Yes." I said, "That was the state patrol." He said, "Yes." "And you were behind me and you are a state patrol and I am speeding? You must have had another reason." He said, "Well, I'll tell you what it is. A big drug shipment came in down there in Corpus Christi and it's going on across into Arkansas and we're on patrol trying to catch it." I said, "Well, I don't have any of it." He said, "Do you have any objection to my searching your automobile?" Well, now here we are, sir, they didn't have a search warrant or anything. I knew the law about that but I wanted to get on home because I was going to California the next day. I said, "No, I have no objection." So I let him open the trunk and he looked in there. Of course, he didn't find anything. I said, "You know, I'm a preacher. I'm a preacher and I don't deal in that stuff." He says, "You're a preacher? They deal in it too."

Our credibility has gone down. Why is that? Why is it that folks do not respect ministers? I think that we have lost our credibility because we've lost the impact of the holy, a sense of a call. God called me to this and said, "This is holy business!" There's nothing holy now for some folks. Isaiah said, "In the year that King Uzziah died, I saw the Lord sitting on a throne, high and lofty....And I said: 'Woe is me! I am lost'....Then I heard the voice of the Lord saying, 'Whom shall I send, and who will go for us?' And I said, 'Here am I; send me!'" (Isaiah 6:1a,5a,8).

Our credibility has gone down because of a lack of Bible knowledge. We do not know our Scripture. Study your Bible. That's what the apostle told us to do. "Do your best to present yourself to God as one approved by him, a worker who has no need to be ashamed, rightly explaining the word of truth" (2 Timothy 2:15). Now since you know that's what's causing the loss of credibility, it looks like you'd want to do something about it. Study your Bible.

A change in the moral climate has made us as preachers lose our credibility. We sing, "Everybody's doing it, doing it, doing it, everybody's doing it, doing it, doing it." But the song doesn't say, "All of the preachers are doing it, doing it." That isn't what it says. The moral climate has dropped down. I know we sin, but you do not have to wallow around in your sin. There is change in the moral climate around you. There was a time when a man standing in God's house knew better than to offer a godly man a drink of whiskey. Now our credibility has gone down because we as leaders *ape* the culture rather than *shape* the culture. We ape the culture. Preacher boy with rings in his nose, ear-bobs, called himself a preacher. I was out at Chapman College in California, saw one of our reverends out there. He said, "Reverend Dickson, you don't remember me, do you?" I said, "I did before you put an earring on." You don't have to act the fool because everybody else is acting the fool. You're supposed to shape the culture. You see a little boy going wrong, straighten him out. Don't be aping the culture.

There is a lack of creativity in our philosophy and in our theology and in our witness. No creativity. You've been riding in a buggy so long, you don't want to ride in a car. Huh uh. You've been riding in a car so long, you don't want to ride in an airplane. You've been riding in an airplane so long, you don't want to ride a missile. You're not creative. You let a deacon or an elder say, "We've been doing it like this for twenty years and you just got here and you're gonna change this?" You lost your credibility 'cause you're not creative. Your theology is about God so you find a way to tell about it. Tell about Jesus. New ways. Open up your mind. Tell of a philosophy that is the starting point of the reality of the cosmos. It's the reality of what God has done. And I'm here to tell you, philosophers rule the world politically. They are the thinker-uppers. We're lost because we are not creative.

All right, we also like fervent preaching. Now fervent preaching isn't 3-S preaching. Now you can do some 3-S preaching: spit, stomp, and squeal. But what we're talking about is *believing what you preach.*You might also do some Y-P-J preaching: yelling, pounding, and jumping. But you still have to say something. I don't care how you jump, you still have to say something. Fervently, *fervently* declare the truth! That's what you've got to do. And that's why we've lost our creativity, because of a lack of fervent preaching! *Saying* something. You can jump all you want to, but you gotta *say* something. You can pound all you want to, but you gotta *say* something. You can run all you want to, but you gotta *say* something. We have lost our credibility because we don't say anything. Fervent preaching. You've got to believe what you're preaching.

Our credibility has gone down because of a lack of meeting the needs of people. Our compassionate core cannot stand as a preacher. And therefore our credibility went down. I was in Edinburgh, Scotland, walking down the street, and a beggar stopped and asked me, "Won't you give me five dollars 'cause I want to get breakfast?" I said, "Come on and go with me and we'll go get our breakfast. I don't know where breakfast is but we'll go on down to the police and he'll tell us." "We don't want to go down there," he said. "Are you a preacher?" I said, "Yes." He said, "I should have known better than to ask a preacher."

We have lost our compassionate core. That's why credibility has gone down. You could always get help from the preacher. If he had one little slice of bread he would share it with you. If he had just a heel, he would share it with you. If he lived in the country he'd go down to the bank or to the store and make arrangements for you, but now if you're asking for a dollar, he'll say, "Sign this paper here, 'cause I want a mortgage on your hat."

Credibility has gone down because of personal sins and attitudes. Yes, personal sins and attitudes. Sins have gotten us into trouble. Bible folk got into trouble too. Abraham lied. Moses killed a man. But that's not your example. David took a man's wife. That's not your example. But your credibility is going down because of your personal sins. And you have to get yourself straight. Get yourself straight.

Our credibility is going down because of infighting between preachers. Preachers fighting each other. Belonging to the same denomination, fighting each other. Belonging to the other denominations and fighting between them. We're all God's preachers and we're saved in the Lord Jesus Christ and you're fighting in here. I'm here to tell you, we lost our credibility because of that. Stop that fighting and let's get together, let's cooperate. Let's belong to each other. Every preacher in the city ought to belong to the other preacher in the city. That's where we are.

Now the other side of it is, the church must change its attitude and stop beating us down. Stop the church from changing its attitude about the minister and build him up. Lift your minister up. Lift the minister up. Do not cut down your preacher. Protect your preacher. Care for your preacher.

See to it. If one man can take care of a ninety-thousand-dollar house, it seems to me that forty families can take care of one family.

Do not major in your sins. David committed sin but he didn't major in it. He asked the Lord for forgiveness. That's what I'm talking about. Don't major in your sins. Moses didn't major in his sin. Abraham didn't major in his sin. Do not major in your sins. Major in your conversion in Christ Jesus. Paul told lies. Paul was at the stoning of Stephen. But he didn't major in that. He used up a lot of the pages of the New Testament telling about how he was converted. "On that note, O King, I was converted." Major in your conversion to Jesus Christ, not in your sins. For though your sins be as scarlet, they shall be whiter than snow. It's cold out there. One way we can get our credibility back is each one policing herself and himself. Police yourself. If you don't, somebody else will police you.

Preachers are the biggest gossips. They tell all the secrets of the members. But if we're gonna get our credibility back, we've got to be confidential. People will be willing to trust us— that's what I'm talking about.

All our hope is built on Christian leadership. It was Christian leadership that brought us all the way. Go back to our history: it was Christian leadership that did it, Christian leadership that brought this country through. And if you're a Christian leader, you're on the right track. It was Christian leadership that brought us out of slavery. It was Christian leadership that took us into emancipation. It was Christian leadership that brought us out of segregation.

So the thing for you to do is go down there and take Faith Street. There's a street called Faith. F-a-i-t-h. Yes, turn on Faith Street where it runs into Hope Avenue. Build your hope on things eternal and hold to God's unchanging hand. Turn right from Hope Avenue onto Love Boulevard and keep on walking. Run on.

Remember, it's Christian leadership that brought us out. It wasn't a lawyer, it wasn't a doctor. It was Christian leadership that showed us the way.

You see, we're a peculiar people. When God freed the Hebrews they got away from Pharaoh, but when God freed us we stayed right here. Our old masters had to learn to get along with us and we had to learn how to get along with them.

Share in administration. Share in employment. This brother-hood is making progress in employing us, but you gotta share in it. That's what Raymond Brown told us after I had told him this when we marched at our convention twenty-five years ago. He told them that they got to share in the administration of this great church. Ever since that day, we haven't been sharing. Now we begin to drop back. Get ready, we need you, seminarians! Get ready 'cause we need you. Christian leader-ship is the answer to our problem. But keep in mind, keep in mind, that it's Christian leadership that's gonna get us out of here. It's the righteousness of Christ Jesus spread by his people. God bless you!

$\mathcal{W}$hat a Wonderful World!

Jack Sullivan, Jr.

Jack Sullivan is director of racial/ethnic and
multicultural educational ministries in the Division of
Homeland Ministries of the Christian Church (Disciples
of Christ). Formerly pastor of Hill Street Christian Church
in Louisville, Kentucky, Jack has degrees from Ohio
University, Lexington Theological Seminary, and United
Theological Seminary in Dayton, Ohio.

Several years ago, the jazz trumpeter Louis Armstrong presented our society with a wonderful message enclosed in a song. His song was titled, "What a Wonderful World." Every time I hear this song, with its message of hope and optimism, I smile and think to myself, as Armstrong's refrain goes, "what a wonderful world."

Indeed, the world really is wonderful. Through the wonders of my position within our church, I have been blessed to see and visit with many wonderful people in many parts of our country and world. In fact, with the advent of satellite technology, you really don't have to travel around the world to see some of the people of the world, for images of the human story are beamed right into our living rooms. Often, we get to view humanity in its finest forms: moments of celebration, moments of joy. Images of people of different races, cultures, and nations, who take life seriously, and who are willing to make sacrifices as they work for the common good. These are people who inspire me to take life to the highest level, to never lose faith, to keep hope and optimism alive.

Hope and optimism. What precious commodities these are! Imagine how wonderful the world really would be if more of us possessed healthy levels of hope and optimism. The unfortunate truth is that for many people in our country and on this planet, the world really isn't wonderful. Disease, natural disasters, wars, political indifference, oppression, and poverty are robbing large populations of persons daily of any sense of hope, and any spirit of optimism.

Hope and optimism, the twofold ticket to personal and social change. They are the necessary elements for persons to believe in themselves and in others, that somehow, if I am forced to lie down, one day I will sit up; if I can sit up, one day I will stand up; if I can stand up, one day I will walk; and if I can walk, one day I will run! Hope and optimism: the higher society's barriers grow, the higher I will learn to jump. Hope and optimism.

Yes, for many individuals and societies across our globe, the world is not wonderful; hope and optimism are in short supply. Unfortunately, the stream of hopelessness and despair can even be found to have seeped into the consciousness of the faith communities identified as the church, causing us to retreat from the work for individual and societal change, thinking that we really can't make a real difference. Imagine that, the church unable to make a difference in the course of the world!

How unfortunate it is when Christian faith communities lose faith! When people, once identified as salt of the earth, light of the world, lose both taste and visibility. Perhaps faith then becomes for us a private matter, between my God and me, as one church member remarked during a stewardship discussion! Can you imagine that our faith would be a private matter? Maybe this is why a significant number of Christians believe they can stay home and watch TV preachers, live what they think is a moral life, while not ever thinking to worship with their congregation, or engage in any actions which are for the common good.

Such privatization of faith was a problem during the time of Isaiah. It was a time of confusion for the people of Israel, as they had been forced to become well acquainted with defeat and oppression. In the aftermath of this, the faithful attempted to gain favor with God through personal denial, otherwise known as fasting. Yet, the prophet Isaiah knew that making their faith a personal matter, reducing it to a matter of fasting in order to persuade God, was not the way. Isaiah was able to present to Israel a more excellent way to be faithful to God.

In the traumatic year that King Uzziah died, Isaiah received his call from God, to be God's spokesperson, to remind Israel of what it really meant to be faithful. Isaiah informed the people that a true fast involves loving service to humanity, to loose the bonds of wickedness, to undo the thongs of the yoke, to let the oppressed go free, to share their bread with the hungry and to bring the homeless poor into their house, and to clothe the naked. Isaiah informed the people that when they did these things, God's healing presence would be with them, with righteousness leading them, and the glory of the Lord following them.

When I consider this kind of fast, it sort of makes me realize that all of those candy bars I may have sacrificed during Lent may have made me feel good, but in terms of social transformation, what did I really accomplish? In times of crisis it's easy to turn inward.

Isaiah's vision of true fasting, true faithfulness indicates to us that the recovery of hope and even optimism, which leads to social transformation, does not come through our turning inward and embracing a private faith. Instead, this recovery comes when we become engaged in service, in challenging the prevailing attitudes which say, "things can never change." Each time someone says this, we must rise up and say emphatically, "Oh, yes, they can." The Search Institute, a religious think tank in Minneapolis, reported that youth are most likely to stay on the road toward being positive, contributing persons when they and their parents engage in consistent expressions of community service. I would think that such service might do the parents some good, too. Clearly, all who would embark upon the path to service may be best able to see how wonderful our world really is.

The fast of service and social transformation is one which many members of our church and other communions have chosen to accept, and the evidence of this has been given to us today. Today we have learned about the work of the church in

places where many of us may never visit. Today we have
learned of God's healing presence throughout the world and in
our own country. From the support of schools and new church
establishment in southern Africa, to the work for dignity and
justice in Latin and Central America, Disciples are engaged in
mission. From rural segments of our country affected by both
drought and flooding, to urban areas afflicted by poverty and
injustice, Disciples are engaged in mission. The more I see
and hear of these fasts of service by our fellow Disciples and
their colleagues from other communions, I am more convinced
that our faith is not a private matter, but a matter which calls
us to give the very best of ourselves for the common good. And
when we do this, more and more, we realize just how wonderful this world really is.

I've been blessed to walk to school structures in southern
Africa which have been supported through our outreach giving, called Basic Mission Finance. I even experienced my own
call to fasting, my own call to ministry through my work in an
inner city mission project at National City Christian Church,
Washington, D.C., funded by our Reconciliation giving. Perhaps you have experienced the church in mission in other
places, or right here in Decatur. If you have, then you know
that in spite of the problems of our world, through engage-
ment, we still believe that this still is and can still be a
wonderful world.

As we both fund and engage in mission together, perhaps
some of the doomsayers may accuse us of being strivers of
some sort of utopia. Well, to that I would say yes, we are,
because we have been able to redefine what utopia is. Rather
than seeing utopia as a perfect society and world, theologian
Karen Lebaqz calls us to view utopia as a society in which we
realize that hatred, injustice, poverty, and oppression don't
have to exist. Once we realize that they don't have to exist, our
efforts at mission can dismantle them, and more people will
be able to experience this world as being wonderful.

A couple of nights ago, the temperature dropped to the
mid-forties, quite cooler than it has been all summer. As we
prepared for bed, I approached the thermostat in our hallway.
I knew that we would not need the air conditioner! In fact, I
thought that we might need to turn on the furnace. Before I
turned it on, I thought to check the furnace to see if the pilot
was lit. If the pilot was not lit, it would be impossible for it to

engage the furnace in the production of heat for our house. Well, I discovered that the pilot had blown out. Yet, I was so sleepy that I decided that we could live with the cool air, and so I left the pilot unlit.

God has given each of us gifts and skills which serve as the resources which, when used properly, can light the pilot light of social transformation and healing. We have the gifts of hope, love, peace, joy, vision, all the necessary ingredients to transform our society, through our collective work for the common good. May we never allow ourselves, through the privatization of our faith, to become too sleepy to use our gifts to serve as the pilot that engages the best of humanity's resolve to become engaged in the work which can transform human lives, particularly those in the margins of life. We've got so much to share. We've got so much to share we just can't keep it to ourselves. May we remember that when we work together, we are never alone.

Pass it on in spite of lower numbers, odds against you, limited resources. Pass it on—we're resurrection people!

*F*rom Paternalism to Partnership

John Richard Foulkes, Sr.

John Foulkes serves the Christian Church (Disciples of Christ) as its deputy general minister and vice president for inclusive ministries, and as administrative secretary of the National Convocation. He previously pastored Parkway Gardens Christian Church in Chicago, Illinois. John has degrees fom Chicago State University and McCormick Theological Seminary.

Philemon

The witnessing of a marriage ceremony always gives opportunity for reflection upon the intimate relationships between human beings. This service of establishing the covenant of the most intimate relationship experienced by humans coupled with the growing epidemic divorce rate and the genocide of the African-American family forces us to struggle with the issue of intimacy and egocentrism. Intimacy binds one's sense of self with another. Egocentrism finds one's sense of self within oneself.

Analysis of Jesus' identification of the greatest commandment in Matthew 22:36–40 supports the current therapeutic focus on self-love enabling love of others and God. The excess of self-love noted in the "I wills" of Isaiah 14:12–15 identifies the evil that can be present in excessive egocentrism. Reflection on the temptation narrative in Matthew 4 heightens this stress when it is realized that the basis for the temptations was the exaltation of self-will above partnership with God.

If an ambiguous relationship exists between healthy self-love and love of the other, there is a critical need for clarity about the boundaries of that ambiguity. In this age of cultural self-definition and struggle for holistic pluralistic community, the egocentric/intimacy argument takes on heightened importance. The question becomes, "Do we have, as our basic motive, *maternalism / paternalism* or *partnership* as we seek relationships with others?"

The most explicit instruction that I am aware of in the word of God on this issue is that found in Paul's letter to Philemon. Let's look closely at that instruction.

The letter opens with the image of a runaway slave, Onesimus, standing at the door of his slave owner, Philemon, with a letter from Paul in his hand. First-century law identified a slave as property and allowed the slave owner to treat that property any way that the slave owner wanted to. The slave owner could kill the slave at will without any criticism or question by the larger society.

Onesimus had not only run away from Philemon but had "wronged" (verse 18) Philemon and was considered "useless" (verse 11) to Philemon. Death would have been expected. The only thing that separated Onesimus from this sudden unquestioned death was the letter that he held in his hand.

Onesimus stood in this perilous position out of an understanding of a new relationship with his slave owner. Philemon was a Christian who had been brought to faith in Jesus Christ through the witness of the apostle Paul—Philemon owed Paul "even [his] own self" (verse 19). Philemon had become a "coworker"(verse 1) with Paul, had a "church" in his own house (verse 2) and had become known throughout the region for his "love for all the saints and [his] faith toward the Lord Jesus" (verse 5).

This special relationship between Paul and Philemon placed Paul in a position of authority as Philemon's mentor. As his mentor Paul was responsible for enabling/empowering Philemon. Paul could have based his mentoring on a system of wise, benevolent paternalism. Paul could have mentored Philemon based on what he had done for Philemon—"I am bold enough in Christ to command you to do your duty" (verse 8). Paul could have made a demand as: Philemon's agent of redemption from the God-limited existence; the mentoring/ instructor of the faith; the counselor that enabled leadership of the church in Philemon's home; co-signer of the notoriety that Philemon was experiencing. Paul, however, chose a higher motivation for the partnership—"I would rather appeal to you on the basis of love" (verse 9).

African-American congregations initially began in the Christian Church (Disciples of Christ) at the close of the Civil War through either missionary activity by Anglo Americans or as a result of separation of African Americans from previously integrated congregations. That same motivation of liberating into self-determined yet segregated existence led to the establishment of African-American educational institutions and even a partnership between those educational institutions and the newly established congregations for the education of ministers to lead those congregations and to start new ones.

Dynamics that are relatively young in the cultural development of African Americans have called for a change of self-understanding from that of being "objects of mission" to "partners in the mission." That shifting dynamic forces the agent of the missionary enterprise to consider, just as Paul had to consider with his relationship with Philemon, do we predicate our future relationship on the paternalistic enablement of the past or "on the basis of love"?

A psychological system known as "transactional analysis" is predicated on three levels of communication—parent, adult, child. Communication can exist between any of the levels. Normal communication between the majority American culture and the African-American culture is that of the parent (majority culture) communicating with the child (African-American culture). When the "child" demands to be communicated with as an "adult" the motivation for the changed communication model by both the former "child" and the former "parent" must be "on the basis of love."

Onesimus, aware of the new relationship that he had with Philemon and Paul's advocacy based on love, holds his physical life in the message of the letter that he holds in his hand. Verses 10 through 12 of the letter make it very obvious that Paul loved Onesimus: "I am appealing to you for my child, Onesimus, whose father I have become during my imprisonment. Formerly he was useless to you, but now he is indeed useful both to you and to me. I am sending him, that is, my own heart, back to you."

Paul refers to Onesimus as "my child," "my own heart," one "I wanted to keep" but, "I am sending him...to you." In his commitment of the giving of what he loved to enable a greater partnership "on the basis of love," Paul must have had a glimpse of the divine love that enabled God to give God's self for humankind that was still in the midst of rebellion against God.

> For God so loved the world that he gave his only Son, so that everyone who believes in him may not perish but may have eternal life.
>
> John 3:16

> But God proves his love for us in that while we still were sinners Christ died for us.
>
> Romans 5:8

God gave his only begotten Son to die for our sins to enable a new partnership—a partnership based on true, honest, uncompromising love for one another.

It is easy to love someone that is "right" by one's own standards. It takes a whole different kind of love, partnership love, to love one who is radically different from the perceived "right."

As Onesimus stood at Philemon's door with the letter in his hand he must have considered the reason that Paul had sent him back to Philemon. Paul must have met Onesimus as an inconspicuous person on a Roman street over one hundred miles from Philemon's house. After having established a relationship with Onesimus, having been an instrument of bringing Onesimus to faith in Christ Jesus and having experienced Onesimus' care, he could have told Onesimus to keep on running. A rationale could have been developed to support Onesimus' not returning to Philemon because of the possible consequences of his escape and violation of Philemon. But Onesimus knew that Paul had introduced him to a new freedom—a freedom in Christ Jesus. This new freedom elevated Onesimus above his social/economic status and gave him a new basis for relationship. "On the basis of love" Philemon was no longer his slave master but his brother in Christ.

Persons of African descent in America know all too well the dehumanization of the marginalized position fostered upon them by the majority American culture. Christian faith, which was developed by and sustains this African-American culture, is so precious to African-Americans that there is great reluctance to seriously share it or allow it to become vulnerable in the majority American culture. Paul's counsel to marginalized African Americans is the same as was given to Onesimus, "I am sending him...back to you....No longer as a slave but more than a slave, a beloved brother" (verses 12,16a). We can't really be free until we go back into the garbage and proclaim our freedom in spite of the garbage.

When Paul and Onesimus came to this basic understanding of liberation in spite of the garbage, some great things began to happen. Paul's love for Onesimus led Paul to intercede for Onesimus. It was love that made Paul stand with Onesimus who was obviously "one of the least of these" (Matthew 25:40) and on the basis of societal norms, wrong. Intercession may occur for many different reasons but only an intercession "on the basis of love" enables a substitution of the intercessor on behalf of the one being interceded for. Listen to the language that Paul uses:

> So if you consider me your partner, welcome him as you would welcome me. If he has wronged you in any way, or owes you anything, charge that to my account.
>
> Philemon 17–18

Paul tells Philemon that he wants Philemon to receive Onesimus as if he were Paul. That slave standing in front of you, Philemon; that person that ran away from you, Philemon; that person that wronged you, Philemon; that person that you could legally kill, Philemon; receive him as if he were me and if he owes you anything, put it on my account. If you need to have the money back, I will repay it. If he is in trouble, I will stand for him.

> God sent forth God's Son into the world that he might stand in our place for sin's sake.

> For our sake he made him to be sin who knew no sin, so that in him we might become the righteousness of God.
>
> 2 Corinthians 5:21

> Then Jesus said, "Father, forgive them; for they do not know what they are doing." And they cast lots to divide his clothing.
>
> Luke 23:34

Jesus said, in effect, I have loved them and interceded for them to the extent that I have given the best that I have—I have substituted myself for them. They can now stand with each other, substituting themselves for each other. They can now be truly liberated and liberating people.

The implications of the intercession through substitution is that we are going to have to take those cantankerous, no-Christian-living, no-Christian-talking folk—you know, those folk that meet in board meeting once a month, those folk that won't do right no matter what you do, those folk that you wonder if they ever even heard about the word *Christian*, those thorns in your flesh, those folk that wouldn't say anything good about you if you paid them—you are going to have to take those folk, substitute yourself in their situation and in the midst of the garbage that they are pouring out toward you, substitute love—and you may not even be able to let them know that you are doing it. You may even find that if they find out that you are trying to love them they may do something else to aggravate that love. But Christ's substitution for you compels you to love them anyhow.

Intercession brought substitution and that substitution brought about restoration. "Perhaps this is the reason he was separated from you for a while, so that you might have him back forever" (verse 15). The psalmist wrote:

I waited patiently for the LORD;
    he inclined to me and heard my cry.
He drew me up from the desolate pit,
    out of the miry bog,
and set my feet upon a rock,
    making my steps secure.
He put a new song in my mouth,
    a song of praise to our God.
Many will see and fear,
    and put their trust in the LORD.

Psalm 40:1–3

Praise be unto God for the substitution. The restoration takes place because of the substitution. If you have been present with others in the midst of their garbage, you can be an agent for lifting them out of that garbage. You can move them from their stumbling and ever falling deeper into the garbage to being placed on a solid rock on which they can stand. Have you ever tried to get a firm footing on mud? If so you know that it is not only impossible but that all of your energy is drained even as you try to stand. The Jesus that rescued us from the miry clay gives us a ministry of rescuing others.

> From now on, therefore, we regard no one from a human point of view; even though we once knew Christ from a human point of view, we know him no longer in that way. So if anyone is in Christ, there is a new creation: everything old has passed away; see, everything has become new! All this is from God, who reconciled us to himself through Christ, and has given us the ministry of reconciliation; that is, in Christ God was reconciling the world to himself, not counting their trespasses against them, and entrusting the message of reconciliation to us.
>
> 2 Corinthians 5:16–19

We are going to have to reach down into some miry clay pits, pull out some people, set them on some solid places and tell them to stand there. Substitution enabled elevation:

> Perhaps this is the reason he was separated from you for a while, so that you might have him back forever, no longer as a slave but more than a slave, a beloved brother—especially to me but how much more to you, both in the flesh and in the Lord.
>
> Philemon 15–16

Intercession "on the basis of love" grows out of the sharing of one's own journey and the desire for another to have that same experience of liberation. The writer of 1 John put it this way: "We declare to you what we have seen and heard so that you also may have fellowship with us; and truly our fellowship is with the Father and with his Son Jesus Christ" (1 John 1:3). The elevation that grows out of the intercession and substitution "on the basis of love" is one of true partnership. There is a new sense of partnership similar to what Christ has enabled for all believers. Paul wrote to the Roman church regarding this new relationship. He stated, "For you did not receive a spirit of slavery to fall back into fear, but you have received a spirit of adoption. When we cry, 'Abba! Father!' it is that very Spirit bearing witness with our spirit that we are children of

God, and if children, then heirs, heirs of God and joint heirs with Christ—if, in fact, we suffer with him so that we may also be glorified with him" (Romans 8:15–17).

The psalmist wrote, "He put a new song in my mouth." I am not singing about the garbage or the mud pit anymore, I am singing about the firmness of the place on which I stand.

Reflect on the struggles that have taken place in your life and the pits that you have found yourself struggling in. Then think about how good it has been to get all cleaned up. You don't feel like the same person.

Have you ever come into the house after mowing the lawn or playing basketball, all sweaty and not smelling like your deodorant is supposed to make you smell? If you then jumped into the shower or tub and washed all of that result of extreme exertion off you, you can recall feeling like a new person. You have reached down and taken yourself out of the mud experience. Jesus took you out of the spiritual muds of your life and placed your foot on a solid rock. Do you know of sisters or brothers who are still in the mud pits? If so, do you feel comfortable standing on a solid rock while your sister or brother is still in the mud pit?

Articles that I read speak of the increased progress of the African-American middle class. Those same articles speak of the recent development in America of an African-American "under class"—persons who are so deeply entrenched in poverty and oppression that they have no hope of ever being liberated.

Some of us have been elevated. We drive pretty cars, live in nice homes, wear nice suits and dresses, have a few shirts in the drawer. We generally feel good about ourselves and often forget about our brothers and sisters that have been pushed so far down that they have become hopeless. The strange thing is that if those who think they have arrived would compare the best African-American-owned business with the businesses listed on the "Fortune 500" list we would realize that we have not even begun to be in the same ballpark. Do we possibly feel good because we look good only because there is someone else who doesn't look as good?

Several years ago, I did some research in education and found that it was difficult for a teacher who is only one generation away from poverty to teach children still in poverty. The newly liberated teacher is aware of the pain and hurt of being in poverty and sets up artificial barriers to intimacy with the poor students.

There are different ways of being liberated from being a victim. One way is to be able to identify someone that is in a worse position than you are and therefore feel good about where you are. Another way is to image a better place and create fantasy about that better place. Living in those fantasies may enable a sense of liberation. Still another way is to imagine a better place to be and set goals to get there. Liberation begins in the midst of the journey. The person goaled in liberation may still be enslaved socially and economically but is free because of the striving for the better place. Jesus' statement of mission in Luke 4:18–19 enables this goaled liberation. Jesus stated, "The Spirit of the Lord is upon me, because he has anointed me to bring good news to the poor. He has sent me to proclaim release to the captives and recovery of sight to the blind, to let the oppressed go free, to proclaim the year of the Lord's favor." I have not found New Testament evidence of Jesus having changed the social/economic status of persons but many evidences of Jesus' having changed victims into nonvictims.

Substitution brought about elevation. "He put a new song in my mouth, a song of praise to our God." I've got something to talk about. I can praise God, not because everything is going well for me but because, in the midst of my garbage, I've moved from being a victim to being a nonvictim. Although I might stand all dirty and filthy, the filth I stand in does not have to be who I am.

Paul said to Philemon, "Listen, Phil, there was a slave that ran away, there's a brother coming back. I could demand some things from you because I am in a parental relationship with you. I don't want to ask as a parent. I want to function with you as a partner. I am not interested in paternalism anymore, Philemon. I am interested in partnership."

African-American members of the Christian Church (Disciples of Christ), we have to let go of paternalism and struggle for partnership. He may have left as a servant but Phil, Oney is coming back as a brother!!

> There is no longer Jew or Greek, there is no longer slave or free, there is no longer male and female; for all of you are one in Christ Jesus.
>
> Galatians 3:28

*T*hese Sayings of Mine

Ozark Range, Sr.

Ozark Range has been the director of Black ministry in the Division of Homeland Ministries of the Christian Church (Disciples of Christ) since 1977. A Mississippi native, Ozark is a graduate of Southern Christian Institute and Christian Theological Seminary.

Matthew 7:24*

"Therefore whosoever heareth these sayings of mine, and doeth them, I will liken him unto a wise man, which built his house upon a rock."

Matthew 7:24

Jesus concluded his Sermon on the Mount with the parable of two builders. The vast multitude that heard him represented a cross section of humanity across the centuries. Human nature never changes. His whole sermon had for its theme our attitudes toward others and our attitudes toward God. After all, the word *beatitudes* means the right outlook upon life. His sermon that day was timely and timeless. It applied to all ages and

---

*The scripture references in this sermon are from the King James Version of the Bible.

spoke to the needs of every heart. The Bible says that Jesus saw them as sheep without a shepherd, and he had compassion upon them. In his message he stressed character and conduct, and his illustrations were concrete and to the point.

The crowd listened to his sermon with great interest. They hung upon every word that fell from his lips; but he told them, as he tells us, that it is not enough to listen. Intent listening must be put into action. We must heed his words and put them into practice if we are to reap real benefits from them. Jesus concluded that sermon with the parable of two builders and said to the masses, "Whosoever heareth these sayings of mine, and doeth them, I will liken him unto a wise man, which built his house upon a rock."

All of us are builders, and Jesus divided us into two groups: the wise and the unwise. Jesus was constantly dividing people into two groups. Here he is saying that all of us are builders, but some are putting some very shoddy material into our building. We often take shortcuts, but there are no shortcuts in building character. We need to build characters that will stand the test of storms. For sooner or later every life will be tested. Oliver Wendell Holmes expressed a noble ideal for each builder in these familiar lines in the last verse of "The Chambered Nautilus":

Build thee more stately mansions, O my soul
As the swift seasons roll!
Leave thy low vaulted past!
Let each new temple, nobler than the last,
Shut thee from heaven with a dome more vast,
Till at length thou art free,
Leaving thine outgrown shell by life's unresting sea.

Christ tells us in the Sermon on the Mount that it is upon his great teachings and the gospel that the life of humanity and nations stand. The fool lives for appearances; the saga searches for secret strength. The wise man will follow the teachings of Christ.

The story is told of a rich man who engaged a builder to build "the finest house that you have ever dreamed of building." No expense was to be spared. The builder was well pleased with his work until the rich man said, "The house is yours, but you must live in it." Then the shoddy materials and blotches that he had made stared him in the face. It was then that he realized how much better he could have built. A man must live in what he builds. Notice in the parable: the house built on the sands fell. People who just live any old way and are content therein just build on the surface.

The words of Jesus, "These sayings of mine," can be classified under two relationships: the relationship we have with each other and the relationship we have with God. Now let us take a look at those sayings that have to do with our conduct toward each other.

The first one is the "Golden Rule." It was not original with Jesus; Confucius had taught it in a negative form centuries before Christ was born; and the Old Testament had likewise taught it in that form. But Jesus lifted it up anew and gave it a positive setting. "Do unto others as you would have them do unto you." The Golden Rule tells us how to live with our neighbors. So often we bungle human relationships. Sometimes we take undue advantage of others. We have never learned the fine art of getting along with others. It is impossible to practice the Golden Rule without a personal devotion to Christ. The one who says "I have no need of religion as I try to live by the Golden Rule" has missed the whole meaning of the Golden Rule. We must be motivated by the love of Christ if we are to practice the Golden Rule. All human need is implied in this rule. If there were no needs, there would be no need for the rule. We need more than shelter, food, and clothing; we need strength, understanding, and forgiveness. We need to be treated as if there was something in us beyond price, despite our foibles and shortcomings. No one can live alone; we need each other, and we need God.

Again Jesus said to the crowd and to us, "Judge not that ye be not judged." Here he was condemning a common practice among all of us. Let us call these petty judgments of others "nit-picking" or finding fault with others. Someone has said that the best way to find out a woman's faults is to brag on her to her best friend, and she will agree with all that you say, and the chances are she will say, "Yes, but did you know that she leaves the sink full of dirty dishes?" or something similar. Jesus speaks out against our hasty judgments of others. Harsh criticism has a way of backfiring on us. Jesus said, "With what ye judge ye shall be judged." It is true that when we sit in judgment on others we are judging ourselves. If we frown at life, it will frown at us. Life has a way of giving back what we put into it. If you put a question mark after the name of others, they will in turn question your motives. There is an old adage that is true: "Chickens always come home to roost." The favorite pastime of these "nitpickers" is to find fault with others. Don't you just love those people who, regardless of how spic and span you may look, take a great delight in brushing off a small particle of dandruff on your sleeve or pick a hair off your collar? A wag once remarked that "a strange hair on the collar makes the fur fly." When Jesus said, "Judge not," it was not good advice to be considered but a command to be obeyed. Finding fault with others blinds us to our own faults and shortcomings. The critical spirit nourishes our pride and leads to self-complacency and makes repentance impossible. It is true that we are measured by our own yardstick. That friend who helped you to pick a neighbor to pieces yesterday may help another pick you to pieces today. Kindness begets kindness; love begets love; and by the same token, hate begets hate.

In the Lord's Prayer which was given in his teachings on the mount, Jesus taught us to pray, "Forgive our trespasses as we forgive those who trespass against us." Paul could preach the doctrine of forgiveness, but he had a hard time practicing forgiveness of others. God can forgive us only to the extent that we are willing to forgive each other. We must have a concern for their rights and privileges if we are to protect our own rights and privileges. You cannot walk roughshod over others without hurting yourself. If we have self-respect, we will have respect for others. Now, these sayings of Jesus dealt upon motives that govern our conduct. All of our actions should be motivated by love.

Again Jesus said, "Take heed," and this time he was warning us against making a show of our religion. We must never seek the praise or applause of others by our religious deeds. A prayer should never be judged by its eloquent language, but it should be judged by the quality of its sincerity. Much of our praying is just nagging God for small petty favors, and sometimes they sound like a *Pathe News* weekly, using them to tell God all about what is going on in the world as though God didn't already know. Real praying is opening the doors of your heart to Christ, who will enter the minute you fling it open.

When Jesus said, "Lay up for yourselves treasures in heaven," he was telling us that you can't take it with you. If we hoard our money here, we will lose it sooner or later. The wealth that you hold today will slip through your fingers tomorrow. Your coffin will hold no safety deposit boxes, and there will be no pockets in your burial shroud. Hoarding wealth means a grasping, greedy spirit, but people will often trade the abiding values for the transient values of life. Among other things Christianity is a sharing religion. When we give to others, we are sending our wealth on ahead. Our Lord was deeply concerned about our attitude toward money, and three-fourths of his sayings had to do directly or indirectly with our use of money. For money is pent-up power. He said that where our treasure is there will our hearts be also.

Human life has an upward, as well as an outward, reach. Jesus said that we cannot serve two masters. We were made for homage, and that loyalty cannot be divided. We cannot serve God and mammon. For it is impossible to serve and please two masters. To fulfill our destiny each of us must find our master. We have the right to choose whom we will serve. The power to choose is our inherent right. Through life there is a broad road, and there is a narrow way. It is up to us which road we will take. Some people try to go off in all directions and get nowhere fast; they just go in circles. To defer a duty is to end with a sense of irresponsibility.

Again Jesus said, "Seek ye first the kingdom of God and all of its righteousness and all these things shall be added unto you." Now may I ask what comes first with you? What do you want most out of life? These are pertinent questions that we must face up to. Just what are the priorities in your life? Then Jesus tells us not to be anxious; in other words, don't get all worked up about things. The person who is always in a stew will develop ulcers sooner or later. The best policy is to just keep cool. In worry, desire fights against desire, and life becomes full of tensions. A bit of grit gets into our bearings, and this produces friction. To fret and stew, fume and fuss, is deadly dangerous, for worry will take its toll of our physical strength. It always puts a strain on our nervous system. But sometimes we become the victim of the tyranny of things. There are three classes of worry: those that are past; those that we dread; and the ones that we now have. God is not dead, and he is deeply concerned about us. We are taught in the Bible to cast our care upon the Lord for he careth for us. I like the Forty-sixth Psalm, "God is our refuge and strength, a very present help in trouble." The psalmist was crying out in the midst of a great upheaval when he wrote those familiar lines. We are to trust in the Lord. I like what the old Indian fighter said on the frontier, "Trust in the Lord and keep your powder dry." We should make an effort to capitalize on our troubles. Faith in God will help us to face our troubles and master them. Thereby sickness can be turned into sympathy and sorrow into insight. The trouble with a lot of people is that they borrow trouble and in brooding over it drain away their strength. It is said that ants pick a carcass cleaner than a lion. Little things worry us more than great crises. Our fretful attitude will bring on an anxiety neurosis. To kneel before God in complete surrender is the best cure for care. Jesus said, "Don't worry about tomorrow, as thy days so shall thy strength be."

Or again he spoke of the straight and narrow way that leads to heaven, which means there must be certain restraints thrown around our lives and that we must learn how to discipline our desires. Paul said, "Lay aside every weight and burden that would so easily beset us and run with patience the race that is set before us." The athlete must keep certain training rules and keep himself physically fit if he is to star in the game. So we must discipline ourselves for the race of life, or we will become religious dropouts. If you will live the right kind of life here in your relationships to others and to God, you will have no fear about the hereafter. Salvation has a two-fold meaning: to be saved from something, and to be saved to something. We are known by the fruits that we bear, and an evil tree cannot bear good fruit, said Jesus.

We are to give more than lip service to the kingdom of God. Jesus said that "Not everyone that sayeth Lord, Lord shall enter the kingdom of heaven." Our text puts the emphasis on two verbs of action, *heareth* and *doeth*. If we live by these sayings, we will be able to stand the test of time when it comes. The house will hold up under the stress and storms of life. The Sermon on the Mount dealt with our attitude toward God and each other. His audience represented a cross section of humanity. He was speaking to the ages. Therefore, let us strive to put into practice both the letter and spirit of these sayings. Amen.

$\mathcal{T}$hrough This Portal

K. David Cole

K. David Cole is pastor of Swope Parkway United
Christian Church in Kansas City, Missouri. The grandson
of a pioneer preacher in the Christian Church, he has
studied at Winston-Salem Teachers College, Lincoln
Bible Seminary, and Brite Divinity School. K. David
recently served a two-year term as moderator of the
Christian Church (Disciples of Christ).

Ephesians 1:3–10

In this message I will endeavor to do two things. One
comes very naturally. The other is a bit more demanding. I
want to share with you—as honestly, as openly, as candidly as
I possibly can—where I am in my faith journey. For me, that
is a given in preaching. And then, hopefully, I will help to
stretch our minds and challenge our faith a bit to where and
to what God is calling us in the now of our existence.

Let it be fully understood that I am not so naive as to dare
even to think that in the allotted time I have—or, for that
matter, in any length of time—I could give discourses that fully
comprehend the grand purpose of God in history. I can only say
that this is very much like the mythical dog of literature who
spent long, lonely hours chasing his tale without ever catching
it. Because of his chase, his muscles were strengthened, his
lungs expanded, and in general he became a healthier and

stronger animal. So with us: our finite minds can never fully grasp the mind of the infinite. But we will be the better for it from our struggles with the meanings from the mind of God.

So let us listen to selected verses from our biblical text. Using the suggestion of Dr. Fred Craddock, let us try to "overhear the words spanning the distance and the time." As best we can, let us lay aside excess theological baggage and seek to hear what that first-century faith community heard.

The consensus is that when Paul wrote this letter he was in prison in Rome, awaiting trial before Nero—waiting for his accusers to come with their bleak faces, their venomous hatred, and their malicious charges. What does one see from a prison cell? Chains? Prison walls, locked doors, prison guards? I would argue that it depends on what's in the person. You perhaps remember the question the little boy put to his elder: "What makes a firefly light?" "It's the stuff that's in him," came the reply. Paul sees only incidentally that he is a prisoner of Rome. He is a prisoner for Christ. From the gloom of his prison he sends a light that has guided and cheered the steps of multitudes.

We move past the greeting and enter this epistle through a magnificent gateway, beginning with the words, "Blessed be the God and Father of our Lord Jesus Christ." On through verse 14 the apostle in his thanksgiving surveys the entire course of the revelation of grace. He looks backward to the course of our salvation when it lay as a silent thought in the mind of God, and forward to the hour when it shall have accomplished its promise and achieved our redemption.

One scholar has suggested that this passage (1:3–14) is one of the most sublime of utterances, an overture worthy of the composition it introduces, a piece of thought-music wherein is sung the glory of redeeming love in its *past design,* its *present bestowments,* and its *future fruition.* It is the song of the universe in which heaven and earth take responsive parts. It is not so much a reasoned statement as a lyrical song of praise. Paul's mind goes on and on because gift after gift and wonder after wonder from God passes before his eyes. What rich material for study!

But for our purposes today, we move to verses 9 and 10:

With all wisdom and insight [God] has made known to us the mystery of his will, according to his good pleasure that he set forth in Christ, as a plan for the fullness of time, to gather up all things in him, things in heaven and things on earth.

God has made known to us the mystery of his will. The New Testament uses the word *mystery* in a special sense. It is not something mysterious in the sense that it is hard to understand, but rather it is something that has long been kept a secret and has now been revealed. What was this mystery? It was this good news that history is not a closed system, that God's purpose is being worked out "to gather up all things in him, things in heaven and things on earth," and this good news is open to all. It is God's purpose that all the many different strands, all the warring elements of the world, should be gathered into one in Jesus Christ. It is Paul's thesis that Jesus died to bring all the discordant elements of the universe into one, to wipe out the separation, to reconcile each with the other and all of us with God. The *grand purpose of God*.

Through this portal Paul enters into his faith life—no, not a mere walking down to become a member of an institution, however important that may be; not a mere signing of a commitment card, whatever that may mean—but through *this* portal, this sense that God in Christ has revealed his purpose for all of history, that history is not "a tale told by an idiot, full of sound and fury and signifying nothing" but an arena for which God has a purpose and a meaning, revealed in Jesus Christ: *through this portal* Paul walks in faith.

I was not there. I could have been there. I was invited to go but, to my lasting regret, I did not go. How I have wished I had been there—in our nation's capitol, in the shadows of the symbols of this great nation of ours when Dr. Martin Luther King looked *through these portals* and shared with us his vision, a vision kindred to Paul's. He envisioned a time when this nation would rise up and live out its destiny, a time when deserts of hate and exploitation would be transformed into oases of love, a time when Blacks and Whites, Jews and Gentiles, Protestants and Catholics would be able to join hands and sing in the words of the old spiritual, "Free at last, free at last, thank God Almighty we are free at last."

I wish I could have felt something of the dynamics, the enthusiasm, the depth of commitment. But I wasn't there. I remember reading of another scene: Jesus, nearing the end of his earthly ministry, praying, "I ask not only on behalf of these, but also on behalf of those who will believe in me through their word, that they may all be one" (John 17:20). I was not there either. But I am not here simply to lament my not having been there. What I wish to do is to challenge us to see through the portal this grand purpose to which God in history is still moving.

It is the Christian conviction that history is the working out of the will of God, that history can be redeemed but is not self-redeeming. It is redeemable because human life is more than an incidental quantity in the balance of nature. It has meaning and purpose, and as Christians we participate in that history as players, not as pawns.

Contrast this noble concept that is the portal through which we see our faith commitment with such words as these. Dr. G. N. Clark, in his inauguration at Cambridge University, said, "There is no secret, no plan in history, to be discovered. I do not believe that any future consummation could make sense of all the irrationalities of the preceding ages. If it could not explain them, still less could it justify them." Andre Maurois said, "The universe is indifferent. Who created it? Why are we here on this puny mud heap spinning in infinite space? I have not the slightest idea and I am convinced that no one else has the least idea either." And the pop tune says, "Whatever will be, will be...."

Many are mired in this concept of history, both outside and (may God have mercy!) within the church. It has produced what Rollo May called "neurotic anxiety": the anxiety of violence and insecurity, a pathological madness that takes persons of reason and reduces them to beasts. It represses and inhibits whatever demands creative expression.

In his book *Include Me Out*, Dr. Colin Morris makes this arresting assertion: "I am not so much concerned about the death of the church as I am about what it is killing." A great deal has been written and spoken about what some see as the impending death of mainline denominations. Some have taken recent figures and projected the year when we as a denomination will cease to exist. Our loss of numerical strength must be a cause of concern and we must address this reality. I suggest that our approach to this reality is merely a Band-Aid approach unless we are willing to grapple seriously with what is killing us. Through these past forty-plus years it has been my privilege to serve as pastor to local congregations and well as in the area, regional, and general manifestations of the Christian Church and my observation is that we have lost our vision of the meaning and purpose of the people of God. The dreams we have are far too small.

"Son, what in the world are you doing?" Those words are etched in my mind from my childhood days, for I often heard them from my dad. There was usually a note of judgment in them, and he was usually right. And so God asks, "Children, what in the world are you doing?" Our answer: going to church, attending committee meetings, sharing fellowship dinners.... "But child, I have called you to walk through history with me, to stand in the face of bloody history and shape it."

I sat last Easter Sunday morning and listened as the choir sang the anthem, "Open Our Eyes": "Thou hast made death glorious and triumphant, for through its portals we enter into the presence of the living God." I thought of the prayer of our Lord, "And this is eternal life, that they may know you, the only true God, and Jesus Christ whom you have sent" (John 17:3). You see, the grand purpose of God does not end in physical death, for God has greater things in store for us. Amen.

$\mathcal{Y}$ou Still Have Time

Shirley Prince

Shirley Prince is an associate minister at Mississippi Boulevard Christian Church in Memphis, Tennessee. She is a graduate of Memphis Theological Seminary.

Joel 1:4; 2:25*

That which the palmerworm hath left hath the locust eaten; and that which the locust hath left hath the cankerworm eaten; and that which the cankerworm hath left hath the caterpillar eaten.

And I will restore to you the years that the locust hath eaten, the cankerworm, and the caterpillar, and the palmerworm, my great army which I sent among you. And ye shall eat in plenty, and be satisfied, and praise the name of the LORD your God, that has dealt wonderfully with you: and my people shall never be ashamed.

---

*The scripture references in this sermon are from the King James Version of the Bible.

There's a continuing theme that runs throughout Scripture and it's the theme of restoration. Over and over again, restoration comes to the forefront. Restoration that returns someone to a former position, a former status, a former condition, is seen over and over in Holy Writ.

There in the book of Genesis, restoration is the theme. The very God who created all of creation walked in the cool of the day and asked of his pinnacle of creation, "Where art thou?" Now, I don't believe God was asking Adam about a geographical location. I believe that God who flung the very universe into existence, who knew all about Adam's downsittings and Adam's uprisings, already knew Adam had committed a dastardly deed. And when God looked at Adam in the cool of the day and asked, "Adam, where art thou?" a process of restoration had already begun. For God more than anyone else knew where Adam was. Whenever we are in a position where God has to ask one of us, "Where are you?" we stand in need of restoration. When God has to question not just our physical existence but our spiritual meaning, and when God searches for one of us, even in the cool of the day and says, "Where art thou?" we stand in need of restoration.

Not only Genesis but the entire Bible is replete with examples of our need for restoration. Restoration comes again and again to all of humankind. It was a moment of restoration when God hung a rainbow in the sky and communed with Noah; that was a moment of divine restoration. When God planted a vineyard and allowed creation to roll on for just a few more millennia, that was a moment of restoration. It was a moment when God looked down upon his creation and saw our sinfulness and had to bring about a flood to wash away our iniquity, and I tell you it was a moment of restoration and we stood in need of being restored. Oh, the Bible is replete with restoration; we need to be restored over and over and over again.

If you don't believe it, why don't you put your ear down to Scripture and ask David about our sin-sick condition? David will say that we stand in need of restoration. It's a constant throughout Scripture that reminds us that there's something wrong inside of creation—that it's not out there in the luminous other but it's somehow inside of *me,* and *I* stand in need of restoration. If you don't believe it, ask King David. Oh, sometime when you get idle in your mind and you find yourself standing on a rooftop—there's nothing wrong with standing on a rooftop, but when your eye catches sight of another man's wife and then you're in a position to take another man's life, I can tell you we stand in need of restoration. If you don't believe it, you just bend down to the Scriptures and ask David.

I tell you, we stand in need of *restoration* over and over again and when I look at that word restoration I realize that it's just another derivative of the word that's so familiar in our culture today—that word called *recycling*. You see, restoration is just recycling, or restoring to a former position, or returning to what we used to be. And I just stopped by to tell you this morning that we have caused enough problems in our own biosphere and that somehow we have realized that we have got to begin to recycle. We've got to begin to restore. Our lakes are coughing up our garbage back at us. The very air we breath is filled with pollution that we placed there, and any day driving down I-240 you might look over and see a tractor-trailer hauling nuclear waste to God knows whose backyard. I tell you, we are realizing the need for recycling.

God has been restoring and recycling us to our former position. God has been recycling us to a previous condition of oneness with his wholeness. For you see, apart from God, out of step with God, we find ourselves fragmented. Oh, yes, we are, church—we are fragmented this morning. Somebody in here this morning is fragmented. Somebody in here this morning is divided inside. There's nothing more dangerous than internal division. It is sad enough to be estranged from those around you, but when you got internal problems, when you're not satisfied with yourself, when you lie awake way late in the midnight hour and you call up God and say, "God, I don't want anything in particular, I just want to know what's wrong with me—why can't I seem to get in touch with you? It seems there's somebody else on the main line. Father, I know I never get a busy signal when I call you, Father, but I just need to hear from you. I need a moment of restoration—recycle me, God. I need to be recycled, you see, I'm down here in the trash basin of life. Oh, I know I wasn't destined for the dust bin, somehow you made me for eternity but I got comfortable down here."

We stand in need of restoration. We stand in need of getting fixed up inside. Internally there's a problem within us. It seems that we can hardly hold body and mind together. I tell you, we need to be recycled.

We need to be recycled in our relationships at home. Oh, it's easy to come and sit in the Lord's house and say, "Great is thy faithfulness," and sleep with somebody that you don't even speak to. I just want you to know that it's easy to sit in God's house and say, "I love the Lord, he heard my cry," and not be able to speak to your child on the way out the door every morning. I tell you, we stand in need of the recycling process. We need to be fixed. We need to be fine-tuned.

We need to be restored in our relationships as church—the church that's supposed to be the body of Christ, the church where there are more soldiers wounded inside than outside, the church where we are supposed to be a blood-bought body of believers, leaning and depending on each other, able to go to my sister and say, "I'm hurting this morning, I don't feel right, there's something wrong in my life." But we are the church, the body of Christ, and we're busy destroying each other and God says, "You need to be recycled. Don't worry, I'm not gonna let you destroy my planet any more than I'm gonna let you destroy my church." God said, "Upon this rock I'll build my church and the very gates of hell shall not prevail against it."

God says, "I've got a recycling process that you don't know anything about." Among the prophets in the Old Testament, there was a man named Joel. God said, "Joel, I want you to tell 'em, tell 'em ahead of time, Joel, you tell 'em that you're a minor prophet, not that your messages aren't important, but tell 'em that you're a minor prophet because you got a shorter message. It's quick and to the point, tell 'em Joel, Oh, you don't need but three chapters, Joel, you tell 'em. You tell them that I've got a recycling process that they don't understand anything about. Joel, I just want you to tell 'em that the *Lord is coming back.*

"O, it's nothing like the way the Holy Ghost works, it's nothing like the Holy Ghost will put it together. Joel, the Lord is coming back. And when the Lord gets ready to come back there'll be some devastating events going on on this planet. Joel, you tell them that the locusts are gonna eat up everything in sight and not only that but the locust, his larvae, his palmerworm, his cankerworm, the grasshopper will eat up everything in sight." I don't know if you've ever seen a picture of the devastation caused by locusts. When a herd of locusts, a swarm of locusts, a collection of locusts—whatever they're called—when they strip an area there's nothing left. Nothing green is left, there's no vegetation left, there's no bark on the trees left when locusts come through an area.

God said, "Joel, I want you to use the imagery of your own time. In an agrarian society I want you to tell them that they depend on the land for sustenance. They depend upon the fields for food. But you tell them that one day the locust is gonna come and take everything away. And the devastation will be so great that no one will be left. You tell 'em, Joel, you tell 'em that when the locust finishes, all that he leaves is larvae. The cankerworm will come along and devour. Let 'em know that the field will no longer produce, that the herds will die in the middle of the field. Even the strong olive tree will not be able to bear. Joel, you need to tell 'em. You need to tell 'em that the Lord is coming back, but in the meantime, Joel, I want you to let 'em know that it's not right now. I'm gonna put a comma in the middle of that sentence and say, 'The Lord is coming back, but you still have time.' So tell 'em, Joel, the Lord is coming back."

Make no mistake about it, church, the Lord is coming back! I know some of you've got your passport down here. Some of you've got your Visa down here. But this isn't home, this is just passing through. The Lord is coming back and, church, you still, you still have time. What kind of God is this? God said, "Tell 'em, Joel. Tell 'em about the devastation that's coming, tell 'em they still have time, tell 'em that I'm such a good God, such a merciful God that I'm no shorter than my word, that all they have to do is cry out and repent and turn around again. I know they need to be recycled, Joel, so you tell 'em that the year that the locust has eaten I will restore it." What kind of God is this? "In spite of the devastation I'm able to restore it. I'll fix it for 'em."

Locusts come into many areas of our lives. The image here for Joel is one of the eschaton—the end of time. There's an even deeper message here, for we know what it's like to have years that have been eaten away by the locust, eaten away by the cankerworm and the palmerworm. Have you ever wasted time, church? Precious commodity, time. Can't be bought with money. Have you ever wasted time? Have you ever lost a moment in time? Have you ever done something and wished that you could reach back and redo it again? The palmerworm has come to claim a part of your life. Do you have a section in your life that the locust ate up? You know, the years that were wasted not serving the Lord. The years when you didn't have time to come into God's house. Those were years when the palmerworm was in charge of your life. Oh, somebody knows what I'm talking about.

The palmerworm, he's the larvae of the locust, and the locust is the adult. He can do only so much damage but the insidious damage that the larvae can do—palmerworm activity right inside the church. Useless activity. Just existing, just occupying a pew. Talking about the year that the palmerworm caused you to waste, look at a wasted life. Has anybody ever been on drugs? Oh, don't forget you're in a church house. Alcohol still is a drug. I just want you to know that those were years that the palmerworm had destroyed. Have you ever been involved in an illicit relationship? Oh, you don't have to answer, I know we're in the church house, but I just wanted to know, church, that those were years that the locust had destroyed. Have you ever taken anything from anybody that didn't belong to you? Something that you knew wasn't yours? Somebody's husband? Somebody's wife? Somebody's job? Somebody's promotion? Those were years that the locust had eaten up and God said, "Church, you still have time—you still have time."

"Church," God said, "I will restore the year that the cankerworm has eaten. I will restore the year the locust tried to defeat you." Wasted years keep you awake at night worried about what you used to do—God said, "I'll restore it." The worry keeps you up walking the floor all night long—God said, "I will restore it." The pain that you feel, separation caused by sin—God said, "Tell 'em you still have time. I will restore it." God told Joel to tell 'em the Lord is coming back, but you still have time.

Joel, how do you know? But Joel went on to continue that verse. He spoke up for God and said that "in those days I'm gonna pour out my Spirit. Sons and daughters shall prophesy. Old men are gonna have vision. Young men will be dreaming dreams because I'm the Lord, I am coming back. But in the meanwhile, tell 'em that you still have time. Oh, yes, you still have time, you see, because I know about your need for recycling. I know that you're in a pickle. That you made a mess out of your life, that it seems like you just can't get it all together." God said, "Joel, tell 'em that the story is to be continued over in Acts, chapter two, and that the moon hasn't turned red like blood yet and that the moon is not black, sackcloth of ashes, just tell 'em that you still have time!"

How do you have time? Precious commodity, time. No one can make it. No one can take it. God said, "I can, because I know about my creation. I can, because I was there when they failed. I can, because I asked Adam, 'Where are you?'" God said, "I can restore time because I am the Giver of all life, I will restore, I will restore. I can destroy but I will defend." God said, "I will restore years that the locust has eaten and I'll do in my own time, in the fullness of time."

Four hundred years between Malachi and Matthew. Four hundred years until God got ready. Four hundred years until God sent John the Baptist out thundering on the bank of the Jordan, crying "Behold the Lamb of God, taking away the sins of the world." He came to restore the years that the locust had eaten.

And how did he do it? O church, how did he do it? Joel, how did he do it? Joel said, "I don't know. David, how did he do it? How did he do it?" David said, "I don't know. Moses, how did he do it?" Moses said, "It wasn't by the law. I don't know how he did it. Eli, how did he do it?" God said, "I did it through my Son. I did it through Jesus. I did it through the spotless Lamb of God. I did it with my own righteousness. I did it because of my love for a sin-sick creation. I did it, I restored years that the locust had destroyed."

Where did you do it, God? "You're mighty inquisitive today. Don't worry about where I did it, but since you asked, it was at a recycling plant on the hill called Calvary." Church, I tell you, he did it. He did it. We are recycled. We are recycling everything from glass to plastic. We're recycling everything from Styrofoam to paper cups, but God said at a recycling plant on a hill called Calvary, "I recycled it for each and every one of you. I gave a life. I recycled death, turned it into life. I recycled 'em, recycled death into eternal life. I took the years that the locust had eaten up and I restored the people of God."

Tell somebody: *The Lord is coming back, but you still have time.*